One More Train to Ride

One More Train to Ride

THE UNDERGROUND WORLD OF MODERN AMERICAN

HOBOES

CLIFF WILLIAMS (OATS)

INDIANA University Press

Bloomington & Indianapolis

This book is a publication of

Indiana University Press
601 North Morton Street
Bloomington, IN 47404-3797 USA

http://iupress.indiana.edu

Telephone orders	800-842-6796
Fax orders	812-855-7931
Orders by e-mail	iuporder@indiana.edu

Library of Congress Cataloging-in-Publication Data

Williams, Clifford, date
 One more train to ride : the underground world of modern American hoboes / Cliff Williams (Oats).
     p. cm.
Includes bibliographical references.
 ISBN 0-253-34368-2 (cloth) — ISBN 0-253-21652-4 (paper)
 1. Tramps—United States. I. Title.
HV4504.W545 2003
305.5′68—dc21

                                        2003010231

1 2 3 4 5 08 07 06 05 04 03

Not all those who wander are lost.

–J.R.R. Tolkien,
The Fellowship of the Ring

CONTENTS

FOREWORD

GYPSY MOON (JACKIE SCHMIDT)
National Hobo Queen, 1990

I grew up listening to the music and stories of my father, who rode the rails for nearly twenty years before my birth. Later, as an adult, I was blessed with the friendship of many hobo friends. Nothing compares to those nights I spent alongside the rails, sitting by a fire with my hobo comrades! It was not unusual for folks from a nearby town who had heard of our gathering to walk curiously up to our camp. They generally approached with caution, then were taken aback by a ready welcome like the one our hobo patriarch, Steamtrain Maury, often extended: *Pull up a log and have a seat. When the light of the hobo fire shines on your face, you will become a part of our community!*

Have you ever jumped a rattler, evaded a railroad bull, ridden on the porch of a graincar under a star-studded sky, shared a cup of hobo stew with a fellow vagabond, or danced the hobo shuffle around a jungle fire? Probably not. Nevertheless, this book challenges you to step away from the routine of life—away from 8-to-5 jobs, rush hour traffic, 24/7 supermarts, cable TV, and computers—and sit awhile around the legendary hobo fire so that its light can shine on your face. In the following pages, vagabonds of all stripes will weave their memories for you. Old-timers and new-generation hobos alike will share their stories, their songs, their poetry, their culture—and invite you to become a part of their community!

Cliff Williams is affectionately known among the hoboes as Oats. In his many years of listening and learning and caring about the hobo culture, he has gained the respect and friendship of hoboes all across America. He has come to understand that, indeed, hoboes are resourceful, free-spirited, and courageous adventurers, but that they are also skilled craftsmen, artists, carvers, storytellers, orators, historians, philosophers, herbalists, songwriters, and singers. Oats is committed in this book to fostering a clearer understanding of this long-misunderstood American subculture and to preserving these hobo accounts for history.

The 'boes who have contributed to this collection have entrusted Oats with their precious memoirs and their most personal work. And he has, in turn, listened with a sensitive ear and an insightful heart, compiling a revealing book that speaks poignantly about their desire for freedom and about the risks, consequences, joys, and hardships that they endure along the way.

If you have ever felt a spark of wanderlust in your heart, accept the invitation: *Pull up a log, turn the page, and let the fire of the hobo community shine on your face.*

ACKNOWLEDGMENTS

I want to thank those who contributed photos, drawings, poems, and songs; Gypsy Moon for writing a foreword; Kendra Stokes at Indiana University Press for suggesting that I expand the original manuscript; Bryan Almond for assisting with the transcription of the songs; and all the wanderers who have welcomed me as a friend. I would name them here, but the list would be longer than the fifty-three who are in the book. I dedicate this book to them.

All photos were taken by Cliff Williams, except for the following:
New York Slim on page 18 by Adman
Stretch on page 59 by D-Rail
Monikers of Stretch and Shortstop on page 68 by Adman
Shortstop on page 69 by Virginia Lee Hunter
Drawing by Shortstop on page 78 by Virginia Lee Hunter
B on page 82 by Roger Ewing
Oats on page 89 by Collinwood Kid
Nomad on page 89 by Dawn DiVenti
Adman on page 154 by Roger Ewing

INTRODUCTION

"Do people still ride freight trains?" a young acquaintance asked with curiosity and disbelief.

"Yes," I answered. "Some ride for fun, and for some it is a way of life."

"A way of life?" he responded with a quizzical look on his face.

"Yes, like the hoboes of the Depression era. But there aren't nearly as many of them now."

This book is about current railriders, for whom riding freight trains is a way of life. They are still called "hoboes," as they have been since the nineteenth century.

After the Civil War, thousands of former soldiers roamed the country looking for work, many carrying hoes as they made their way from place to place. It is thought that they were known as "hoe boys." Later, during the Depression in the 1920s and 1930s, a new wave of travelers went out looking for work, this time with a different mode of travel. The picture of migratory workers became linked with the image of boxcars filled with desperate men and the sight of campsites—"jungles"—inhabited by those men.

Many people think that the era of the hobo ended with the Depression. In a way, this is true, for the hundreds of thousands of hoboes populating the rails then have dwindled to a couple hundred or so now. Boxcars and jungles were full then. Now it is relatively rare to spot a hobo on a passing freight, and even rarer to stumble across a jungle.

In another way, however, the era of the hobo has not ended. People still live on the rails, moving about by catching freights. They wait for trains under bridges or in wooded areas, sleep in boxcars, and camp in jungles. They work at an array of temporary jobs. And they possess many of the same character traits—they like to go their own way; they do not live within the rules and restrictions of every-day society; they cannot be tamed.

These traits are amply illustrated in the accounts in this book. Frog and Dante just happen to run into trainriders. Within hours they are on a moving freight at the start of a long trainriding career. The only place New York Slim finds that he fits in is out on the rails with fellow travelers. B squats in abandoned buildings. The Texas Madman climbs into a boxcar to avoid being put into an orphanage.

Hoboes are also restless. They are driven by an irresistible need to move. "I have to keep moving," declares New York Grizzly. "Even though I say, 'No, I'll never do this again,' I end up doing it again," New York Slim admits. And Dante asks, in his gravelly yet expressive voice, "You want to leave now? . . . When a train goes by, why don't we just jump on it and go? Where? Where the train goes."

Then and now, hoboes have written poetry, some of which has become songs. In the old jungles, hoboes would build a campfire to cook and stay warm. They sat around it swapping stories of their travels. Sometimes they would play their favorite traveling instru-ment—the harmonica; sometimes a song would burst forth, and sometimes a poem.

The poems in this book represent hoboes' unique traits. "Catchin' Out for Freedom" by Guitar Whitey displays the hobo's aversion to being tied down. "One More Train to Ride" by Hobo Liberty Justice vividly depicts the irresistible impulse to roam. "Softly by Tracks" by Buzz Potter conveys the hobo's love of freedom. "Hobo's Lament" by Virginia Slim shows the hobo's penchant for self-reflection.

The poems also depict experiences typical of hobo life. "Shanty by the Main" by Iowa Blackie describes a hobo's temporary shelter. "Sitting Around Our Little Fires" by Oklahoma Slim describes what happens in jungles. "The Hobo and His Bedroll" by Bo Britt Eddie paints a detailed picture of the hobo's morning routine.

In the life stories, poems, and descriptions of hobo life in this book, you will observe hoboes' daily activities and witness their close encounters with death. You will discover the unique features of vagabonds who have fallen in love with the rails. Here are unfor-gettable pictures of distinctive people who have chosen to live on the outside, both physically and socially. They represent a typical cross-section of railriders. Some have been traveling for more than two decades, some for only a short time; most are older, a few are young; most are male, a couple are female; most are white, two are dark—one African-American and one Dominican. All, however, belong to the deeply subterranean world of the freight train traveler. They like to think of themselves as the elite of society's basement—or as not part of regular society at all.

Adverse publicity over the years has given hoboes a bad name. During the late 1990s, two serial killers frequented the rails, and one rail traveler was on the FBI's ten most wanted list (though he was later cleared of the murder charge). The public perceives railriders with a good deal of wariness and suspicion. At best, they are bums who need to be steered clear of; at worst, they are criminals who need to be locked up.

The material in this book dispels this misconception about rail-riding culture. There are, to be sure, "cockaroaches" and "wingnuts" among those on the road, to use the hobo terms for the bad element in their midst. "Hoboes are criminals in about the same proportion as in regular society," Oklahoma Slim once remarked. But many are friendly and approachable; they would not hurt anyone any more than you or I would. They just don't live the way we do.

I was able to obtain these stories and poems because I have been going to the annual National Hobo Convention in Britt, Iowa, since 1990. I had seen a picture article about the convention, and something in me said, "I have to go there." I did, not just as an observer, but as a vicarious participant, or "hobo at heart," as nonhoboes there are called. I took the name "Oats," because I eat rolled oats with milk and honey for breakfast every day.

Hoboes have been gathering at "conventions" since the nineteenth century. One of the convention songs that George Milburn includes in his 1930 *The Hobo's Hornbook* is about a gathering that took place in Greencastle, Iowa, on May 12, 1890. Those in attendance included Pete the Shive, Boogie Sam, and Old Ring-tail Sykes. The convention at Britt was first held in 1900. It is not the only convention that hoboes have gone to, but it has become the most prominent of them. It now attracts people like me who identify with hobo life even though they have not been full-time rail travelers.

What do hoboes do at a convention? They sit and talk. They trade stories of their travels. They play music and do the "hobo shuffle" around a campfire. They cook and eat—all outside, of course. Being at a hobo convention is like being at a family gathering.

During the annual poetry reading in 1993, after the hoboes had discovered that I am a college professor, Steamtrain Maury Graham—a patriarch of hobo culture—asked me if I would publish some of the poems. I gladly agreed to, founding the Hobo Press in 1994 and publishing two booklets of hobo poetry and one of life stories of current railriders.

The life stories in this book are based on interviews I did at the annual Britt conventions. I have edited the transcripts of the interviews lightly for the sake of readability. Otherwise, the words are just as the hoboes originally spoke them. The sayings that are interspersed among the life stories were collected partly by me and partly by Linda Hughes, who is caretaker of the National Hobo Museum in Britt, Iowa.

A CAUTION

If you are tempted to try riding a freight train, don't. In the words of Nomad, a veteran rider of fifteen years, "Do not do what I do. It's dangerous, it could get you killed; it's illegal, you can go to jail. And you're going to get addicted to it and possibly destroy whatever chance you could have at a real life."

One More Train to Ride

Catchin' Out for Freedom

GUITAR WHITEY

*Hoboes feel shackled when they are living in normal society. Rules
and regulations make them feel imprisoned. "I love being a hobo,
with no schedule and no one else's expectations to live by," The Texas
Madman once declared. Guitar Whitey, who carried a guitar with
him in boxcars and on graincars, expresses this sentiment in the
following song. Now in his early eighties, he traveled full-time
for several years in his twenties, then rode occasionally for the
subsequent fifty years until he stopped in his mid-seventies.*

A hobo's life is happy,
    a hobo's life is free.
It's a life of travelin' all around,
    and that's the life for me.
I'm just a guy that won't fit in,
    I've always been that way.
I'm catchin' out for freedom,
    I'm leavin' today.

A life of endless travel,
    the freight train is the way.
The blue-steel rails are tellin' me:
    go see the U. S. A.
These city shackles bind me,
    how I long to get away.
The highline is callin',
    I'm catchin' out today.

I must have had five hundred jobs,
    my fate has been to fail.
But when the sun comes up each morning,
    I'm heading for the rail.

People call me "just a tramp,"
    a "loser," so they say.
They could be right, I put up no fight,
    I'm happier that way.

I often miss the family life,
    a fireside and a home.
But there's something deep inside of me
    that makes me want to roam.
As the years roll by I wonder why
    I choose the iron rails.
The hobo life keeps calling me
    to follow the hobo trail.

So I'm catchin' out for freedom
    like a never-ending song.
Catchin' out for freedom,
    I've known it all along.
Ever since I could remember,
    I've always been this way.
I'm catchin' out for freedom,
    leaving today.

The Texas Madman

The Texas Madman has been traveling for more than thirty years. For a long time he specialized in crop picking and farm work. After an injury several years ago, he interspersed his traveling by rail with traveling by bicycle for a time, but is back to traveling by rail. He spends his winters in the south and his summers everywhere else, working now and then to keep himself going. He once called me from another state—he was headed toward a city in that state to find work because he was down to five dollars.

Every day is a new adventure.
                                    —Road Hog

I tried settling down, but it got old after a
week.
                                    —The Texas Madman

I started hoboing in 1972. I grew up in a family of hoboes. Mainly my mama was a hobo, and my daddy was a hobo. When my mama got pregnant with me, she settled down, but that didn't make her any the less of a hobo. She still had that spirit in her from when she was traveling and working like she was.

I don't know anything about my mother's hoboing. It was before I was born. I heard about my father's hoboing from my mother, but only the fact that he traveled trains as a migrant farm worker and carpenter and such. Nothing specific.

For a long time I was looking for him out on the rails. I was wondering about him. It was amazing that I found out that he was deported back to Scotland two weeks before I was born. That's why I never saw him around the house. I didn't find that out until a couple of years ago. I used to ask around with folks up in different parts of the country, and I had my suspicions about other folks, other old boys, but it never panned out.

Our whole backyard was filled with hoboes. All year long, bumming season, or working season, or whenever, different migrant laborers were there. See, in the backyard, about forty feet away from the back door of the house, was a train track, and the backyard was known as a regular hobo camp. This was in Lampasas, Texas.

My first hobo experience was right after Mama died in 1972. The county and state wanted to put me in an orphanage. At that time orphanages were the most disgusting places in the world for anybody. The state and the city and the county stated that I had no family, but my family was hoboes. So I contacted some of them, telling them what was going to happen to me. We hit the trains. And I been with my family ever since.

My first experience I had with hoboing, I actually traveled, I think, about a quarter of a mile. I hitchhiked from Lampasas over to Temple, and here was a beautiful Katy railroad train fixing to head out to San Antonio. It was sitting on the line and waiting for a crew. So I go over and slide myself into a boxcar and go to sleep. And I wake up in Temple, the same town, but now I'm no longer on the Katy tracks. The train is a quarter of a mile further over in the Santa Fe yard. That's my first experience. First experience ever.

After that it was about two or three days before I could actually catch another train, another Katy train, out of Temple, because I found a few things in Temple to build up a little money before I headed on down to San Antonio. It was one of the slowest southbounds that they had at that time. It stopped every twenty miles. It never did drop off any equipment, it never did pick up anything, it just stopped, went a little bit further, then twenty miles later it stopped. This was when I was thirteen.

When I got to San Antonio, I worked over at Alamo Iron and Metal. Lied about my age and they believed me. They didn't ask for no ID. Back then they didn't care. Worked over there sorting out steel and cast iron. They were busting it up, getting ready to run it off to the smelter.

I worked there for about a month, month and a half. Got tired of that and got the train back up to Temple. That's when I ran into Cherokee Joe, an old hobo that used to come to Lampasas quite a lot that I'd got to know. He took me and said, "You ever been to

Kansas?" I said, "I've never been out of Texas. This is my first time out of Lampasas." He said, "Come on, we're gonna go ride on the Kansas Pacific." And that was the first time, back in '72, that I got out of the state and went someplace else.

I was with Cherokee Joe for a year and half. I started actually to hit with other old boys that used to come through Lampasas, and I started ranging to other parts of the country. For about a year and half, I traveled with other old boys that I knew came from out of town and slowly got a bit of an education so that I could get off on my own. Then I got off on my own when I was about fifteen. Traveled by myself.

I was given the name Madman because of an attitude and activity in Missouri when I was working in the fields, out in the cabbage fields in Missouri. I was about sixteen. At that time I was working fields on farms and camping out back in the jungles. There were about four or five of us together. We would pick amongst us in the morning, one person. At the end of the day all our money would be pooled together, and the one specific person would go into town and pick up the supplies that we needed to take care of us until the next day.

Well, one day we picked this one individual, and after our work we pooled our money to him and sent him off to town to pick up our supplies. After about three and a half to four hours of him not returning, we decided to go out and look for him. We found him in a beer garden drinking up all our profits and not buying a damn thing. We hauled him on back to the jungle, after stopping at a liquor store, tied him up to a tree, and tried to figure in a democratic manner what punishing to do.

I finally got tired of this democratic discussion, and I grabbed a brake hose and beat this guy. I didn't kill him, though he was quite bloodied up. He was tied to a tree, so there was no way he could defend himself against me. We untied him and told him to get out of the camp and don't ever be seen anywhere again.

After he left, the other individuals said, "We should have had a camera to take pictures of you, because you were making sounds, animal sounds like a mad animal. You had smoke coming out of your ears. From now on when anybody sees you on the road, they'll know you by the name of 'The Texas Madman.'" That's how I got that.

I used to be a crop laborer and do light industry. Now I do a little bit of crop work, light industry, carpentry, replacing window glass, interior painting, exterior painting, interior remodeling, carpet laying, auto body work, diesel mechanics, sand finishing, and needlework—aside from times when I run into little towns where there's nothing around and I got to do a little bumming.

Everybody has those dry days. You can't say you worked hard every one of your days out here on the road. There's going to be some of those times when you can't find work and you're flat broke and got to do a little bumming. So what? As long as you don't make a career out of bumming.

I don't think you could say anything could be a typical day, because in my life every day is a new adventure. There isn't really anything that is much of a typical day. I wake up in the morning, I'm alive. I get up and start moving. Eventually, I drink coffee to wake up with. Then I look at the sky. I say, "It's a good day. It's a good day to live. It's a good day to die, and I'm ready for either one." Then I go about my business.

When I'm out traveling, I usually sleep on the train, right in the yard, right in a section where I can find cars being repaired by the car shop. I get in one I know is not going to be moving any time in the next three or four days. The main thing is looking specifically for a boxcar. The main reason for that is to be able to sprawl out, but also for the fact that overnight, should a nasty storm come in and rain, I have the roof over my head, plus overnight you get a lot of morning dew, and it takes forever for my sleeping bag to dry out.

In the winter times past I used to travel all around, but the past five or six winters I've put down for, like, three or four months. For the past couple of years I've spent my winters on the Gulf Coast. When I first started traveling, I traveled in the south and in the north. But my health's getting down. I've lived hard for twenty-seven years. And I can't do at forty-three what I used to do at fifteen to twenty-five. I can't do it. My body's shot. I can't endure certain amounts of rainy weather and cold. Not like I used to. I'm getting old.

Everybody gets tired, and your body is not going to stay young forever. It's going to start aging. You're going to have aches and pains. I can't keep this up on a steady basis anymore like I used to, all year round. But I don't think I'm ever going to lose the desire to wander—the desire to wander and work and to meet other people. I don't think I'm ever going to lose the love of traveling on trains. I don't ever think I'm going to lose the ability to get up and do like I'm doing now. I just ain't going to do it on a regular, daily basis like I have been.

Sometime down the road it's gonna be cut off to, say, about six months on, six months off. But so what? There's no one rule or regulation that says a person has to hobo and travel trains and work and such every dadburn day of your life. There's no law putting it down there, unless you personally have the mindset that that's your own personal regulation upon yourself.

A recent experience I had was going out to Washington, D.C., July 4. I had been invited out to D.C. years and years and years. Well, I finally took my friend up on his invitation to come out to spend some time with his family and go to the memorial services, the Fourth of July services at the Vietnam Veterans Memorial. He also invited me to the big fireworks display by the U.S. Marine Corps out in Quantico. So I called him up and I said, "Well, look, I'm in Chicago. I'm going to come on out. You give me about four or five days to get from where I'm at now out to Alexandria."

So I got on this train, and it finally left out, I think it was about 7:30 that night, and slowly made its way through Chicago. It started getting dark. I just went to sleep, because I didn't see all the areas that we went through as we got out of Chicago. By the next morning, about 6:00, they pulled into their first crew change in Garrett, Indiana. I got off the train, because I had already been on it, I figured, about twenty hours. Too slow—it'd take me too long just to get to Willard. I got off in Garrett and went out and had me some breakfast at a little café—it's a railroad café. It's called the B & O Café, because it's the old B & O route going through Garrett and on into Willard.

I got done with my breakfast and I went right back down to the tracks. Just perfect, right then and there, here pulled in a container train. I didn't have to get off this thing once until we got to Baltimore. It went right through Willard, had a crew change, right through New Castle, Pennsylvania, had a crew change, then went on into Baltimore, Maryland, first Philly, then over into Baltimore. Got off at Baltimore. All on a doublestack. Picture perfect. No railroad police. Got off the yard real quick.

I went out and caught a bus to town, a city bus. Got the Greyhound bus out of there and went on down to Washington. I know some of the train yards in D.C., and once you get inside the yard there's no escaping the railroad police or anything else. So I got on a Greyhound bus, going through D.C., ending up in downtown Alexandria. I got there on the third of July. So I spent the third, the fourth, and the fifth at Alexandria, in D.C., and down at Quantico.

Leaving out of there, my friend decided he was going to have to take Amtrak up to Philadelphia. He said, "I'll pay for another Amtrak ticket, you ride up to Philly, and I'll leave you." That was free, getting out of there. It was the first ride on Amtrak I ever made. And it'll be the last ride I reckon I'll make on Amtrak. It was too much like riding a Greyhound bus. I'm a smoker, and they wouldn't let me smoke anyplace except the club car. I won't go into the club car, because I have a tendency, once I get around all that liquor, to phsssssss. I get real fluid and will not get on a train if I'm plastered. After that point, I stayed out of the club car until we got to Philly.

Out at Philly I went back over to the yard. It took me about three hours to catch out on a stack train back up to New Castle, P.A. It pulled up to a stop to do another crew change in New Castle, and I got off again and went over and got a little grub. The stack train pulled into a little stop, and another general merchandise train is sitting there. They pulled the power off the stack train. So I asked them what they're doing. They said, "This train's staying here."

"Well, what about this other one, this one with the fridge?"

"Oh, it's going on."

So I went over and got on to an empty boxcar on this GM train going out of New Castle and sat there. And the train sat there. The train sat there for another hour, then two hours, then three hours. Four hours later, I got off and I found the switchman and I asked him, "Now hold it. You said this train was going to be going out of here pretty soon. I been sitting on it for four hours. What's wrong?"

He said, "Pittsburgh and Lake Erie Railroad operates the CSX route out of Lake Erie, down through New Castle and going into Pittsburgh now. So what they did, they came down the hill into New Castle with a two hundred and seventy-nine-carload train full of taconite"—that's tiny little steel pellets. "They hit a curve that's rated for fifteen miles an hour going thirty miles an hour, and dumped a hundred and seventy-six carloads of taconite along with the cars, tearing up at least a quarter to a half a mile of track and ties."

So I asked him, "How long do you think it's going to take," 'cause I know that this is a trunk route. They got to get this route open, because they got to rail trunk freight into Chicago and back over to Baltimore way. "How long do you think it'll take for them to rebuild this?"

He said, "Maybe you're looking at anywhere from twenty hours to two days." I said, "Well, I'm not pressed for time now, and I got a little bit of cash on me and I can take care of myself." He says, "Okay, just show me where you're at, and I'll come wandering out and tell you when we're going to be moving."

I was stuck there a total of eighteen hours. Had to set up my teepee, because nine hours of that was in total gully-washing downpour.

They finally got the route open, and as we're climbing up the hill at three miles an hour—after a derailment, a freight going up there is going to be slow—going around that one curve, I saw the derailment took out the double track main. We had only one track open now. The other track was totally demolished. And here were a hundred and seventy-six cars all pushed over the hill, heading on down into the gorge, and a whole bunch of tiny steel pellets. It looked like a bunch of marbles, like somebody dumped out a super huge Godzilla-sized bag full of marbles all over the place.

I finally got out of there, went back in through the town of Willard, which is a major three-mile-long train yard. The train I came in on busted up there. It took me about six hours to make connections to another train going on into Chicago. I went through five cans of mosquito spray gettin' rid of mosquitoes. If you know Willard, it's sitting out there on a dry lake bed. It's old black swamps out there. It had been raining through there, and mosquitoes were out the yin yang. I got out of Willard, finally, back through Garrett, and back into Chicago. Now I know to stay away from travel on taconite trains, especially on Pittsburgh and Lake Erie.

As to whether it is harder or easier to travel, it's not so much that it's harder as it is that I'm more leery of certain places, as opposed to the old days when I would just boldly say, "Hey! It doesn't matter what's what and who's who, I'm going." But nowadays I'm just a little bit more leery of certain areas. I travel by myself. I don't carry weapons with me. In certain areas I've found out that there's continuous violent activity mounting up. I tend to avoid those areas. It hasn't gotten harder for me to travel. Just certain areas I will not travel in.

I don't have anything to prove to myself or to anybody else by going to those areas and facing that violence off. I don't have anything to prove by that. So if I don't have anything to prove by that, why go there? That's somebody else's idea of adventure. I have no need to go there and have that adventure. I don't have any desire for it, and I don't have nothing to prove by going through it. So why do it?

I like smaller towns. I don't poke into dinky old poke holes in the road, maybe fifty thousand people. But I like my smaller towns. Smaller and littler medium-sized towns and biggie places, I can always find more interesting things to do and things to see than I can going to these major, neon, flashy cracky holes.

What keeps me going is a desire to exercise my federally protected—while they're still federally protected—civil right to free movement, free movement in this country without the requirement of license, censure, registration, and regulation. That's what it says, expanded, in the United States Bill of Rights.

What keeps me traveling is enjoying my life, enjoying it the way I been doing. I've had a nine-to-five lifestyle. Time and time again I've tried a nine-to-five lifestyle. I could do it for two or three months, but it gets to be monotonous after a while. Nine times out of ten, I get used to the job. It gets to be boring and monotonous. I can't stand monotony. I have to have an adventure. On the rails I have an adventure.

Then the people that I live around, not only are they wondering where I live, but they're constantly, in a figurative sense, peeking in the windows or something like that, constantly wanting to pick me apart, wondering what I'm doing, and trying to run my life. But it's my life. When I'm in town working, fine. Somebody can run the job. When I'm off work and at home, it's my life. And no one's got a right to stick their nose into my affairs.

I been traveling by train up until last year, when I said, "No more trains, I'm going to go by bicycle." I been riding my bicycle since the middle of February 1999. The two main reasons for this are, one, over the years trains quit doing the shorter crew changes and went longer and longer distances. Where I traveled around to, there were a lot of little places that I wanted to get off the train and just poke my nose in and see what's going on. I couldn't do it when you're traveling two hundred miles to another crew change. So this affords me to drive thirty miles, forty miles, maybe fifty miles a day, but stop at every dinky little poke hole in the road.

The second reason is, after this operation, this hip operation I went through this past winter, my doctor said it was very advisable for me to take at least one year off of railroading while this operation in the hip and the muscles firm up, get their exercise. So I'm taking his advice.

I carry about forty pounds of belongings on the bicycle. I have two pairs of pants, two shirts, two pairs of socks, and one hat. This hat is the old cornstripe I had last year. I decided I wanted to keep it. Cutting the holes in it like this is like air conditioning. It's actually a lot more comfortable than a full engineer's cap like this originally was. And rather than going out to try and buy another six-dollar hat—just cover it up and make your own.

Now I have a tent, but I very seldom set it up, unless I'm going to be setting down at a gathering or some other place where I'm going to be working for more than a day, say two days, four days, six days. If I'm gonna overnight, that tent is staying inside the rat rug, because it takes forever to set it up, then it takes forever to take it back down.

I will admit one thing—the years that I've traveled without a tent, and now that I'm traveling with a tent, I don't see how I got along without it. That has been one of the biggest helps I've ever had in my life. When you want to escape mosquitoes or deerflies that are biting at certain times of the year, it's wonderful. Oh, yeah.

It's better than building a fire with old railroad ties and getting the nasty smoke all over you. The smoke gets rid of bugs, but it does no good for you to try to use that as deodorant or cologne. It's definitely not cologne or deodorant. And it takes a long time to wash it out of your skin. It takes forever to wash it out of your clothes, and if you've had that continuous heavy smoke in your clothes for a long time, burn 'em and go get some new ones, because you'll never get it out.

I never counted the miles I rode. I never bothered to count over the past twenty-seven years. But given an estimate, I probably averaged about thirty thousand miles a year. Some years I might have done maybe six or seven thousand miles. Some years I might have ended up doing a hundred thousand. I don't know. I was never one to count every dadburn mile marker on the road and tally up everything, because I was never one of those to sit there and brag, "Oh, I got this many miles. Oh, I got this many miles. Let's keep up with Mr. Jones and beat him!" No, no, I ain't in a race with nobody for mileage.

Traveling means to me, for work and for pleasure and for the fact that it's home. It is not to be in a contest or a race or for a certain status symbol. Basically it is home. It is transportation across the country, and it is for enjoyment. And of course it is for work, too. That's it. I have never been sucked into that mentality that I've got to be a mileage freak, a speed demon, and try to be better than anybody else because I rode this train and I rode this type and I rode under this way.

What Is a Hobo?

The dictionary defines a hobo as a migratory worker. When you come into contact with real hoboes, though, you realize there is more to it than that. What more it is, however, is difficult for outsiders to say. Here are descriptions by a number of insiders.

A hobo is a person who chooses to live a wanderlust lifestyle with no regrets. —FROG

A hobo is someone who rides trains, that's all they really do, someone who travels around by freight, gets work when they can, and doesn't ever settle down in one place. —DIANA

A hobo is someone who isn't committed to one certain job, someone who doesn't want to be tied down. They just want to travel, and they work when they have to. —OOPS

Today's hobo is a person of free spirit who has given up worldly possessions in exchange for freedom. A real hobo will work for his stuff. He's not looking for a free handout. He wants no problem from anybody, and he'll give no problem to anybody. Hoboes don't like rules. The only rule they have is respect. —BUCKUP KEN

A bum is a guy who doesn't do anything. He's your local drunk, sitting around on the park bench all the time, feeding the squirrels, pooping in his drawers, and getting drunk, until they get mad at him and run him out of town and he finds another town and he does the same thing. A hobo is a person who travels and works and makes his way as honest as he can. No sticks, no stones, no attachments, nothing to hold him down. —CAPTAIN DINGO™

A hobo is as constant as the ever-changing moon. —SNAPSHOT

The first thing I think of when I think of a hobo is of a guy riding a freight train. People who stow away on ships are called stowaways. People who hitchhike are called hitchhikers. People who ride trains are called hoboes. There's got to be a train involved, not watching them, not loving them—riding them.

There's no difference between a tramp and a hobo. The generation of folks that traveled before me called themselves hoboes. Tramp is just a term that came later. I work all over this country and travel on freight trains, and I'm a tramp. I've known plenty of hoboes that were great beggars, and I've known plenty of tramps that don't do anything but work.   —NEW YORK SLIM

When it's cold outdoors, a tramp takes a newspaper and stuffs it down his shirt to stay warm. A hobo does the same thing, but he reads it first. There's a hierarchy. The difference is in the willingness to work and be self-reliant. Hoboes are the elite of society's basement.   —ADMAN

What Is a Hobo?

I've often been asked what is a hobo.
To answer this will take awhile.
A hobo is a person who exemplifies every type of freedom ever dreamed
Unfettered by time clocks.
He's not under the thumb of a foreman
And his life is not owned by a bank or mortgage company.
The regimented life forced on most people cannot be forced on him.
No man forces him, no man owns him.
He's a wandering wind,
    a gypsy spirit,
    a shooting star,
    a wandering eagle.
His home is anywhere, and nowhere, and he travels from home to home.
His way of travel is however he chooses, on foot, on trains, by bus, by car, by truck, motorcycle,
bicycle.

He makes his way however he can.
He doesn't plan his day, or week, or month, or year.
He's fond of saying yesterday is gone, tomorrow hasn't got
here yet, all I can do is live today,
this very moment, and celebrate life.
He's the working stiff's dream of what he wants to be.
And the working stiff's dreams are the hobo's reality.
What is a hobo?
A hobo is the spirit inside all of us that dares to dream and
live that dream completely!

—THE TEXAS MADMAN

One More Train to Ride

HOBO LIBERTY JUSTICE

*There is always one more train to ride for the hobo. It is as if the
riding itself is the end, and not just a means. This song by Hobo
Liberty Justice, which he has sung at numerous hobo gatherings,
was inspired by Steamtrain Maury Graham, who may well have
traveled a million miles by train. Steamtrain wrote in his* Tales of
the Iron Road *that "a restless inner prodding had sent [him] on
the road at a tender age." Hobo Liberty Justice is a retired trucker
who has traveled on occasion by rail. The music for this song appears
on page 140.*

When I was only twenty-one,
I left my home in Atchison
Via boxcar on the Santa Fe.
Told Mom and Daddy not to grieve,
The time had come for me to leave,
The cinder trail was callin' me away.
But that was forty years ago,
I've rode a million miles or more,
The ramblin' fever still burns deep inside.
I've been in almost every town,
But I could never settle down
I've still got that one more train to ride.

Refrain:
There's one more train to ride
It's comin' round the bend.
Gonna hop that old westbound,
Ride it to my journey's end.
I'd really like to stick around,
But I could never settle down
I've still got that one more train to ride.

When the evening sun goes down,
I'll find a place to lay me down
In some old hobo jungle once again.
But when the train comes by at dawn
It's "So long, pal, I'm movin' on."
I'm goin' somewhere I ain't never been.
And when I make my final run
To that land beyond the sun,
I will hold my head up high with pride.
I'll ride the westbound to the end.
I hope St. Peter lets me in—
I've still got that one more train to ride.

Repeat refrain

New York Slim

New York Slim has been traveling by rail off and on since 1976. He occasionally travels in a pickup truck with a cap on the back. His size and charisma make him a commanding presence, and his warm and friendly smile makes him approachable. He is a natural leader, and other trainriders gravitate to him.

It ain't the miles, it's the smiles
—Mountain Dew

I don't always claim to be right, but if I tell you that a mosquito can pull a plow, hitch it up.
—New York Slim

When I was about eight years old, I was a short, fat kid. I think I was 5'5" and weighed two hundred pounds. Now I am 6'6" and weigh two hundred and fifty pounds. They had me on a diet then. The doctors had told my mother that I couldn't eat because I was grossly over-weight for my height. Everybody else got whole portions of food, and I got half portions. They couldn't figure out why I hadn't lost a pound. The reason was because where we lived, in Binghamton, New York, there was a freight yard, and right adjacent to the freight yard was a hobo jungle. Those guys in the jungle always had a pot cooking.

When I first went into the jungle, I didn't have reason to be there, so I tried to be invisible. They would drive me out, but I hung around and hung around and hung around so much that they got used to me. They'd feed me a couple of times a day every day, plus I was get-ting half portions at home. But there were times when I wouldn't even eat the half portions, I'd get so full in the hobo jungle.

I should tell you a little bit about my uncle. My uncle was a significant father figure in my life. I had a father who worked hard and tried to raise a good child. My father was a busy person; he was a practical man. He worked hard all his life; the only thing he endorsed was working hard. My father was also given to hyperbole. He could stretch the truth a bit much, but my uncle never did.

My uncle was one of the greatest people that I ever met. When he told you something, you knew it was the truth. If he said, "I'll be there on Christmas," well, then I just didn't go to bed. Before midnight he was going to show up. I grew to love him, respect him, cherish him. And all he ever was, was just a raggedy old man.

So I grew up. I went to high school in Mount Vernon, New York. Mount Vernon High School has had more professional basketball players and college-level basketball players come out of it per capita than any other high school in the United States of America. I was a pretty good basketball player, and I got a basketball scholarship at Marquette University. The country was at war in Vietnam, and I got a deferment so I didn't have to go into the military. But because I didn't keep my grades up as I intended, I ended up getting drafted.

In 1969 I went to Woodstock and I thought, "Here's my generation of people." But there was something so different about me, and so different about them, that I knew I just couldn't exist around them. Between '73 and '76, I actually tried to be your average gentleman. But it didn't work. I didn't fit. I didn't belong. I couldn't hold a job. Not one job. Actually, I had many, many, many jobs. I found myself in transit all the time, and I guess that's why they call a transient a transient. I found myself going from one place to another place.

In 1973 I don't really know what had happened, but my uncle wasn't around anymore. He didn't come over anymore. So I visited places. I took off. We were still living in Mount Vernon, New York, at the time, and I took off and went up to Binghamton and was hanging around the old hobo jungle up there. I set out on a quest to find my uncle. At first I did it by hitchhiking, but in 1976 I caught my first freight train.

My first time walking into a yard, I had to be the goofiest young guy in the entire world. There was an old hobo whose name was One-Eyed Boston Blackie who immediately made me feel like a worthless individual, because he said, "Hey, stupid. What are you doing?" I said, "I'm getting out of here. I'm leaving town." He told me, "No, you're not going anywhere. You're gonna hang around here for a couple of days, because you're so stupid you don't even have a water jug."

I knew he was right. And I hung around with him. Actually, I hung around with him for a couple of years. He taught me how to find the train, find what I needed in town, the Salvation Army, all the missions, places that you could eat, places that you could shower. He taught me the angles on getting work.

When I first started riding trains, panhandling and soundflying and all that stuff were completely unheard of. We would start in Florida in the juicing season and end up in the Okanogan Valley in Washington picking apples or up in Upstate New York picking Macintosh apples. That was the route. We didn't go anyplace that you couldn't get work.

He taught me hobo etiquette, rules of the road. He taught me that if you're going to be out here, you need to make these things very much a part of you, because they're real and they're codes that the hoboes live by. With hoboes, you could probably hit one of them on the head and open their skull up and give them a hundred and fifty stitches right across the middle of their face, and they'd forgive you a lot quicker than if you lied to them or stole their bedroll. There are some definite codes, some definite rules, some definite laws and bylaws.

One of the things the tramps today say, and it's one of my mottoes, is "I don't lie, cheat, or steal." The reason I withdrew from the greater society into this microcosm is because everybody lies, cheats, or steals out there. I never ever wanted to live like that. I wanted to live closer to what God intended for man. The only people I've ever found, the only group of people I could ever find, that lived like that were hoboes. That was my earliest experience with hoboes as a child, going to the hobo jungle and getting fed by those guys. I knew from way back then that these guys are honest, these guys are caring, these guys are loving, and I was always destined to be with these people because nobody else in the world seemed to be like that.

It's been a proven fact, in every society, in every race or creed, or whatever, you got your cockaroaches and you got your good people. There are cockaroaches in this world, and there always have been and there probably always will be. But you got real good people in this world with the biggest hearts, the biggest smiles that you'll ever see in your life. And I've been privileged to know some of them.

One-Eyed Boston Blackie had known my uncle, and they had actually been good friends. I had remembered stories that my uncle had told me about Blackie. I actually met Blackie in a mission in Galesburg, Illinois, while hitchhiking around. He told me, "There's no way that you're going to find Butcherman hitchhiking. You want to find your uncle, you got to ride the train." We called my uncle Uncle Butcherman. His friends called him Spike.

Spike was one of those guys who hung out in Minneapolis, Minnesota, in the old hobo jungles. In 1984 he was beat to death. They took a brick at the 37th Street bridge in Minneapolis and beat his brains out. The reason they did it was because they wanted to see a nigger die.

I had been riding all that time since 1976 looking for my uncle. I had been riding in the east, because I didn't know he knew anybody out west. I didn't realize how vast the hobo community, the hobo culture, was. I had no idea. I had no idea that the people I was seeing in Erie, Pennsylvania, were communicating with people in Colton, California, or Yuma, Arizona. I had no idea. I had met these people, but I was kind of quiet and laid-back. I wasn't as outgoing as I am now.

I heard the story about a black guy named Spike who was beat to death in Minneapolis. When I heard that story, I didn't know it was my uncle. I found out on my way west that that person that had gotten beat to death was my uncle, the uncle I had been searching for for all these years.

In 1984 I came to Minneapolis, Minnesota. I met a guy named Leo Brun. I met guys named Art Smart, No Bomb, Dante Fucwha, Shotdown Wills, Spaceman, Preacher Steve, all these guys that had a place called the Hole in the Wall. And I ended up loving these people.

To be honest, when I first met these people, I was very angry because my uncle was one of the Hole in the Wall Gang, and he had been killed. I thought, "If you guys are together and you guys are hanging out, how could you let him be killed?" But I understood. I understood how some things happen and how everything happens for a reason.

I think I've always been a hobo from day one. And I've always been a deeply religious person. I've always been a great believer in God. I believe in Jesus Christ; he is my Lord and Savior. And I believe that my religious studies and my belief in God are another reason that I ended up out here as a hobo.

I was a deacon in the church, and I became a junior elder in the church. The more I stayed in the church, the further away from God I got. And the deeper in the jungle I got, the deeper involved with the people that I live with every day now, the more I found love and God.

I believe that God wants everybody in this world to love everybody in this world. I think we ought to start practicing it and not care about insurance premiums and sitting around and watching television.

I think people ought to relate to people. I don't think everybody ought to trade their cars in for a backpack and come out on the road. But I think that if everybody just loved somebody once a day, that's all, if everybody gave somebody some care, some concern, a smile, we'd have a different world.

When I get into town and walk five miles and I don't know where the mission is and I don't know nothing, and I'm tired and funky, and I'm sweaty, and I ain't got nothin', and some little old lady smiles at me and says, "How you getting along?" it makes my whole day. Now I'm going to have a positive attitude. Now things begin to happen for me. That one person changes your attitude, your attitude changes another's attitude, that changes another's attitude, and here we got a chain reaction of good stuff. That's what I believe in.

My philosophy is that the earliest recorded hobo was Jesus Christ. So I try, I try, and I fall way, way, way, way short, I try to walk in his moccasins. I actually get up in the morning and tell that to myself. Can I make this day like Jesus lived a day in his life? And I fall way short. The first thing I do is light up a cigarette and have a cup of coffee. I fall way, way short. But that's my ultimate goal, and my daily goal is to live each day like you want to go to heaven. If you do that and close your eyes at night and feel like, "Well, I gave it my best shot," then you're going to go to heaven anyway. I believe that.

One of the things that we have to deal with, almost daily sometimes, is when you go to missions and places like that because you're hungry and you need something to eat, they make you sit through a church service in order to eat. A lot of guys out here have a real thing about that. They don't want to hear anything about God, because it's being shoved down their throat. I've heard some of my best friends curse God, not because that's what they've really felt, but because here's somebody shoving it down their mouth. They mean, "Don't make me have to listen to a sermon just to feed me." I think that if Jesus were here, he wouldn't do that.

One of the reasons that I continue to ride freight trains is because of relationships that have developed over the years, with people like Shotdown Wills, with people like Iwegan Rick. We've grown to be very, very close over the years.

It's no secret I hang around with a pretty rough band of coco-nuts. We call ourselves the Tramp Family. Some people call us the FTRA. They call us a bunch of thugs, goon squad, all kinds of stuff. We're the guys that nobody ever wants to come around. People say, "They're the rowdy bunch, they're the drunks, they're the people who cause the problems."

What people don't know is that we really, really love each other. You can see it in everything we do. Some of us are drunk, some of us are loud, and some of us are obnoxious, but when you see us with each other, you know we really love each other. We are really, really willing and open to love anybody who comes into the circle and just sits down.

I don't drink, and everybody says, "How is it that you hang around with these people?" And how it is, is because these are the people that need the most. I'm a giver, and that's where I'm needed. I kind of consider this my mission. I think if you truly believe in God and truly believe in Jesus, it becomes your mission to love somebody and pick out some people to love, and it's the rest of your mission to let those people love you.

People see me as a spokesman for them. Normally that's because I'm the only one who is coherent, so it ended up being my job. If something nuts happens, then here comes the cops, and I'm always right there in the front line. A lot of times I am the go-between because I'm against violence, I'm a pacifist. A lot of times I confront the violent situation within groups, argumentative situations within groups.

The thing is, I don't lie, I don't cheat, I don't steal, and people who do have to stand on their own merit. If you get drunk, if you get arrested, that's your business, and that's happened to you. It's not been my fault. I've attempted to keep things on all sides calm, because that's the type of person I am. But if you allow yourself to do something wrong, then you need to answer for what it is you did that was wrong. But I believe the same for every side, not just for some people. I believe it should be that way for everyone.

There is a big confusion. People think that the people who ride trains don't like the people that don't ride trains. That's not true. We just want them to be honest about who and what they are, because we're honest about who and what we are. You can't love and not be honest. There's no love when there's no trust.

One of the reasons that most people ride trains, why most people hobo, is because they don't fit in. I found the only place in my life that I ever fit is out here. And I'm sure that anybody that's ever done this for any length of time has done it for that reason, because they didn't fit in anywhere else.

Now we have a bunch of kids out riding trains, and nobody wants them because they look different. So who are we to have the same prejudice toward them that drove us to this world? I love the kids. I am one of the biggest advocates of the kids. I was one of those kids who visited the hobo jungles and got fed by those guys. I realize now that those hoboes back then must have seen something in me, the same thing I see in many of the kids.

Everybody is trying to define "hobo," "tramp," "bum." I guess I'm all three, because if I'm hungry I'm gonna ask somebody for some- thing to eat. If I just got into town and it's six o'clock in the evening, you know what, there are no labor pools open. You cannot go and ask for a job. If it's a seven-mile walk across town to go to a jungle where you can lay down and go to sleep, I'll ask somebody for bus fare. I'll beg if I need to beg, I'll work if there is work. I actually love to work. I earned the money to go to the hobo convention in Britt, Iowa, by bucking hay in Helena, Montana.

The guy who bucks the hay is the guy who's got to grab the hay bale and throw it up, and then get up there and stack it after he's tossed it up there. It's not an easy job—eighty-pound bales. Baling hay is different—a machine does that. I can buck hay all day. I'm a fifty-three-year-old man who is in excellent shape.

I'm lucky. I'm fortunate in that I'm a skilled individual. I'm a pretty good carpenter, I can operate heavy equipment, I was a pipe layer in Florida for a few years, and every time I go to Florida I'm into laying pipe. I'm pretty handy with my hands. In fact, I'm the guy that out here on the tracks, if your backpack breaks, everybody brings it to Slim, because Slim will figure out how to fix it. I call it Afro-ingenuity.

Yes, I do get tired of hoboing. There are times that I'm so tired and so utterly fed up—I get on the train, they pull the power off of it, and it drops me off in the middle of the desert somewhere in Texas or Arizona. It's a hundred and fifteen degree heat, and I swear that I'll never, ever ride another train or hitchhike. I'll work, I'll buy a car. But the truth is, it's addictive. It's addictive. Even though I say, "No, I'll never do this again," I end up doing it again.

I've been married three different times—the same woman, just in different bodies. Each time it didn't work, because it was my fault, because I felt this wandering spirit. Each time I felt that if I bought the house near the tracks, then I could hear the trains and I could see the trains go by. Maybe that would be enough. But each time that was too much. I ended up catchin' the train.

I wish I could settle down. I got some people that want me to, some people that love me a lot, and I just can't. And it hurts.

Things are both harder and easier now. Harder, because I'm getting older and slower. Easier, because I'm getting wiser with age. I can remember when I first started riding trains, I wanted everybody in the world to know I was on the train, so I waved—"Hi!" And the police would pull me off at the next town I went through. Now I hide and I make sure no one knows that I'm there, and I don't get pulled off as much.

Trains are getting harder to ride for people that don't know about riding them, but not for people that are veterans. I've always ridden hard trains. I've never run from a fight in my life, regardless of what type of fight it was, a fistfight, any kind of a fight. If they say they don't want me on a freight train, that makes me catch a freight train. I'm not going to lie. A large part of that goal for me is the thrill of knowing that regardless of what they say or do, I'm going to get from point A to point B on a freight train. I'm not going to do it hitchhiking, I'm not going to ride a Greyhound bus.

I've never been in jail for riding. I refuse. I refuse to go to jail for riding the freight trains, so I'm one of those people that, if I get a trespassing ticket, I will either go to court and take care of it or not go back to that town for a long, long time. They call it the get-out-of-town ticket. They can make it hard to ride freights, but it's like cat and mouse. Usually the cat wins. See, the bull, the railroad officer, he's the cat, and you're the mouse. But I always say, have you ever seen Tom and Jerry? Sometimes the mouse wins.

I travel everywhere. I've been in every state in the lower forty-eight, and I got there on a freight train. If you go under a bridge that crosses a railyard in America, somewhere you will find my moniker etched on there. New York Slim. Always movin'.

I prefer to get freights when they're sitting still, back in the yard. The reason I do is because I carry a hundred pounds of gear. When my grub sack is full, it makes forty or fifty pounds in addition to the hundred. I carry Carhartts, snowpacks, all year round, because I do this all year round, because I don't have a place.

Carhartt is a brand name of overalls. Snowpacks are things you wear on your feet. Regular boots are good, even insulated boots. You can get away with zero temperatures with them. But sometimes when you're riding a freight train and that freight train is moving at sixty miles an hour, if it's zero temperature, it's sixty below in your car. So we got to be extra careful to have things like snowpacks. They're almost like mukluks, the things you put on your feet with two-inch-thick wool insulation to keep your feet from freezing. I've been frostbitten before and I almost lost my toes, so I'm real careful about being able to stay warm.

I carry that stuff all year long, because you never know where you're gonna be and when you're gonna end up when it gets cold. There are many places people tell me, people I really trust, "You can leave your winter stuff at my house. You can leave it here and just pick it up." But you never know what part of the country you'll be in, so I take it with me all year round.

I do have a place. I have an acre of land in Havre, Montana, and a friend of mine gave me an acre of land in Spokane, Washington, and my sister has five or six houses. I don't have to do this if I don't want to. But I choose to stay out here, to live out here, all year round, so I got to be equipped to be able to do it. You got to have a stove, you got to have a tent, you got to carry that stuff everywhere you go. It's all my possessions, my house.

My favorite car to ride is a boxcar, because you can hide real well in them, and they're comfortable, usually. The railroads need to do more maintenance on a lot of these boxcars. They shake around too much. They're still my favorite ride. I prefer a boxcar to a grainer, because no matter what the inclement weather is, in a boxcar you can halfway stay dry. My favorite ride for getting there is the container, because normally they move a lot faster than mixed freight trains.

I sleep in my tent, under a bridge, everywhere. We've been doing this long enough so that most of the places that we go, we've been there. So we've located what we call base camps. If I'm in town, I'm going to go find the guys that I normally hang out with.

Of the ten people that I am with right now, that's only a small portion of the amount of people that we actually call our family and ride with all year around the country. I would say that we represent maybe a tenth of the people that we actually socialize with all year long.

I've been discriminated against because of my color by other railriders that have very, very prejudiced agendas. It's been a lot of years that I have been riding trains, and when I first started, blacks couldn't ride the highline. You catch a black on the highline and he's gonna get his butt tore up. So I had to ride the highline. Over the years, and I believe it's because of God in my life, He has used me as a vessel, a tool, as an instrument, to help get rid of that attitude.

What do they say about the FTRA? They're a racist gang of ho-boes. They also say that the head guy in charge of the FTRA is New York Slim. What they don't realize is that New York Slim is a black guy. It's weird.

When I first met these people I now ride with, a lot were racist and prejudiced. It was because they never had a relationship with a black man. And they didn't have a relationship with this black man. But things have changed. Me and Dogman Tony call each other best friends, and he's got a swastika tattooed under his eye. It's one of those things that's happened over the years. And not just with me. Whereas black people couldn't come around some of these guys, now there are black people that get to come all the way in and don't even get judged. I think that that's real important.

What Is It Like to Be
on a Moving Freight Train?

*Seasoned hoboes are so accustomed to riding freights that they rarely
tell you what it is like actually to be on a moving freight. For those
who have never been on a freight train, that is one of the most
intriguing things about being a hobo. Do the train cars shake? How
noisy and windy is it? What does it feel like? Here are several vivid
descriptions.*

After a little while the train starts singing to you. When you're on it
long enough, it sort of makes a noise that's like music. I hear it.

—DIANA

It's dirty, but generally it's a smooth ride. Forty-eights are nice because they got a big spot where you can hide and see all around you.
Boxcars are really jerky. Grainers are pretty nice because they got
a nice porch, and there's a little hole you can hide in. Gondolas are
nice, except that the sun beats down on you a lot.   —OOPS

When I had gotten used to riding on boxcars, I would lay down and
go to sleep. That old car, rocking back and forth, would rock me to
sleep. But when it stopped, I was awake, looking out the door, trying to see a sign of what city I was in. A lot of times I got up early
enough where I could see the city limits sign. Other times I had to
look around to see if I could see the name of a business that might
be the name of the town, like Bakerfield Bakery or Phoenix Feed
Store or something like that.   —HOBO CHARLIE

You're rocking with the steel.   —GRAINCAR GEORGE

You get shook around a lot. Sometimes the train jolts and it feels like it's going to derail. But once you loosen up and realize that's how the train goes, it's okay.   —CORRINA

The thing that hits you first is how big the cars are. From far away, trains don't look big, but when you are on one they make you feel very small. My first time ever I was on the shelf of a graincar right behind the fourth engine. That huge engine swayed as we went down the tracks—you don't see that when you look at engines go past you. It felt as if I was sitting beside a shaking elephant that I could not get away from.

There is lots of noise, but it isn't usually clickity-clack like it used to be, because the rails now are mostly long and welded together. The noise comes from the wheels, but there is also loud clacking that comes from the couplers when the cars jam into each other, which they do a lot. That's called slack action. When the brakes go on, they squeal. The train also squeals when you go around a curve, but it is a different kind of squeal.

Sometimes a wheel is flat, meaning that it isn't perfectly round. When that happens, you hear it real loud. And the car you are on shakes. That doesn't happen too often, but when it does, you wonder why you ride trains. Most of the time, riding is quiet—you get used to the noise, so it feels like it is quiet.

The sound that I don't like is the crunch of the gravel when I am sitting on a train in a yard. It might be a friendly yard worker, or it might be a yard worker who looks friendly but later calls the cop, or it might be the cop coming to kick you off.

Once I was in a boxcar and the rails must have been bad, because that boxcar shook back and forth so bad I thought it was going to go off the tracks. I couldn't stand, so I sat in the middle holding on to the floor, which didn't help much.

I don't like to get on when the train is moving. I have several times, though. That train has no concern for you. It just keeps moving.   —ROADMAN

Roving

GIDEON

The hobo's yearning to rove is symptomatic of a larger spiritual yearning. Many of us are as restless as the hobo, wanting something more, but rarely knowing what finally would satisfy us. Gideon depicts this restlessness sharply and decisively. He is in his early thirties and has traveled and done migrant work off and on since his mid-twenties.

Nowhere, just moving
As life does
The constant drone
Clickity-clack clickity-clack
Immerses my mind
Into a trance
As the miles of green fields
Industrial wastelands
And other scenery flash by
Time stands still
And this magic carpet of steel
Pushes relentlessly ahead
Helping me once again
To find the key to unlock
One of life's many cages
Setting my yearning
Spirit free

Dante Fucwha

Dante is one of a number of hoboes who hit the rails after serving in the military during the Vietnam War. He has slowed down a good deal due to health problems, but continues to ride now and then. His wild hair and long, scraggly beard, though atypical of hoboes, aptly express his way of life.

What I like about being a hobo is that I sleep when I want to sleep, I eat when I want to eat, I work when I want to work, and I don't have to worry about the IRS.

—Uncle Freddie

Next load! Any road!　　　　—New York Ron

As a youth, I hitchhiked around the country. I never wanted what anybody else wanted. If they showed me a book in school, I saw a picture—of the Grand Canyon. So I went to the Grand Canyon to go look at it. I stood out on the grounds. I said, "All right. That's it." I don't know if that's hoboing, but that might be traveling.

I started traveling when I lived in Mexico. One day Sammy said, "Can you do me a favor?" I said, "Yeah, I'll do you a favor." I signed up and went into the military, and they sent me over to Asia. I got to hang around in Asia. I got to hang around in Bangkok and I got to hang around in Singapore, all 'cause of this guy's favor.

Every now and then we'd go down out of the mountains—I'd go up for, like, fourteen, fifteen, sixteen days in a row. We'd walk down and there'd be the railroad tracks. I'd said, "Hey, lookit. We sit here long enough, one's going to come by. I know we can steal it." So we'd steal it. We'd hold the guns up and we'd stop the train. Passenger, freight, whatever. We're not walking any further, and we know exactly where the train's going.

They had a flatbed on front with tons of sandbags so if they hit any mines, it would blow that car up. Then they would fix the train. They always had repair craft on it. We used to steal trucks, too. That was our ride. Got tired of walking. I had just spent sixty days on my feet walking simply in the mud. So that was trains.

Then I came back to America. My mind said, "I'm home, my mom is here, and she's happy to see me." My brothers and sisters, I didn't even know who these people were. I had a sister born when I was gone. My sister hadn't even met me, had no idea who I was. I was somebody that would stab you in the heart without even thinking about it. She was two years old. I'd go to bed and my little sister would climb in bed with me. I didn't even know her and she made me a better person, because here is the innocence of youth climbing over to the foulest person in the world. I'm a baby killer, a drug addict. That's what I got out of being in Vietnam. I been blown up, I been shot down, I got holes in me.

I came home in January, and it was maybe ten degrees below zero. The country I had just left was a hundred and eight degrees above. So I went to live in the south, in Palm Beach, because I wanted the heat and I had some friends there. This was 1971. I was born in 1948.

I was minding my business one day, getting ready to cross the street at the railroad tracks. I was going home, because I worked for a living. I had just gotten a little beer, and I was standing there. There was this old black guy who was standing there, too. I said, "Nice day, isn't it?" and he goes, "Yep." I got a couple of cold beers in my bag, and I'm just walking home, and we got to wait for this train to go by.

This guy said, "You know, fella, we could go anywhere in this country on one of them things." I said, "Okay. If a fella had to go to New York, how would he go about it?" He said, "Well, I'm going to Baltimore. My tent is right over there." And I said, "I live right over there. I'm staying with these people and I'm working for them." He said, "Come on, let's go. You don't need this, you don't need this. You need this, you need this, and you need this. All right, come on."

So I got on the train with him. His name was Socrates. I just jumped on the train with this old black guy. He put the word in my head and we went—not on the train that was passing just then. We waited for another, later that evening. Where I was living, it was a siding, and they always pulled the train over. If you sat there long enough, you could catch a ride.

We got to Baltimore. We're up in the Camden's, and we pulled in and there's a bunch of people in the little jungle. I walked in, and everybody laughed when they see this guy coming—"Hey, Socrates." These are old black guys and some old white guys and just old freight train–riding people. They're rapping when they see you, and there's going to be a good time.

Socrates says, "This is my friend. He's a young kid, his name is Dante Fucwha, and he's got to be in New York." This one guy says, "I'm going to Buffalo." I sat around camp all night, and these people welcomed me better than I had ever been treated by the government or America or whatever. It was like my family, and they didn't even know me.

The next day I ended up going to Buffalo with another crazy old man. I got to my job and I worked, I did my union construction work in Buffalo, New York. I was building nuclear power plants. I was against the idea of clean air; it didn't mean anything to me. They were paying me twenty dollars an hour to be there. I did it.

My mind said, "I rode with these guys, so when I leave, why don't I just go back the exact same way I came?" And I tried that. It didn't work. I ended up in Texas. The next time I rode, I could find my way from Florida to New York to go to work, but I couldn't find my way back home. The next time I ended up in Kansas. The next time I ended up in, like, Oklahoma.

For some reason, somewhere, I don't know exactly where it was, they switched and sent me the other way. I asked, "Which way am I going?" They'd tell me, "That way." I said, "That don't fit my map. I'm going this way." They'd go, "No, you're not. You're going that way." I didn't lose anything. I didn't get where I was going. I *did* get to where I was going, because I got there. I didn't make a mistake, I just didn't go there; but when I finally found it, I said, "Oh, I've been here. I know this place and I can do it again anytime I want."

I went. I got my beer, I got my food, I did whatever I do. I learned this country by freight. It's all in my brain. The map of the country is in my head.

I knew where I could work. You had to survive. I knew where the oranges were, I knew where the watermelon was, I knew where the grapes were, I knew where the apples were, I knew where the wheat was. I could go anywhere in the country to work. Particular seasons. Always by freight, because that's what got you there. My idea was, I wanted the freedom of the travel, of the movement, of the motion.

I know where every liquor store is in every city I've ever been in in this country, and I can get to it. I know what time they close, what time they open. I know where every peanut butter sandwich is in this whole country, from Alabama all the way to Wyoming. I know exactly where to go to get a dollar. I know exactly where to go to get fifty cents. Socrates said, "If you get somewhere, mark it down." I got a black book. My book still works.

I also knew where I could get a job. I knew where I could cut the lawn for somebody; I knew where I could wash the window, wash the car, cut the grass. By the end of the day I had four or five dollars in my pocket, and I was a billionaire, because here comes a five-million-dollar train that would pick me up and drive me where I wanted to go next.

I laughed at midnight on the train, because I got both doors open and aura borealis is going on. That's the northern lights. They're flashing, and I'm sitting there drinking a beer, smoking, "Is there anything better than this?" My point in life is, I loved freedom, because I had been captured and caught by something and I didn't like what it was. The train became my avenue of escape.

I was a POW in Vietnam, but they only had me for three or four days before I decided I didn't like being treated like that and killed every one of our captors. We stole their guns and took their clothes and we left. But it took us one hundred and eighty days to get back to American lines. So freight train riding for me is freedom. I am in charge.

The train is thousands of pounds—it will cut you, it will kill you. I have friends with no arms, no legs, no toes. But if you give it respect, you got it. I'm getting on it, it's going somewhere. I'm going to go over there, anywhere, I really don't care. I got all my space back immediately just by taking a train. Why not? Why not? It's exactly what your soul and your heart needs at the particular moment.

America. I brought my bedroll and I slept underneath f it was raining, I would get underneath a bridge or ere I wouldn't get wet. I slept on the earth that I de- g the ground] This is my bed. It's the ground. This isn't going nowhere. Sitting on the grass, the sky's above us, this is our freedom, this is exactly what I fought for, this is exactly what I wanted.

I ride alone mostly. I don't need the company. I'm hard enough on myself. I really don't need somebody else talking to me. The worst part is that I have to carry my gear all the way to a liquor store to buy my beer and carry it all the way back, instead of having someone watch it, which makes the trip lighter and easier. But I'll go.

A typical day would be, I'm sitting on the side of the railroad tracks and I'm waiting for a train. If it's sunny, I'm getting a suntan. If it's cold, I got a fire. That's a typical day. Or reading a book. What book am I reading? I'm reading Lawrence Ferlinghetti today. I love his poetry. He's a wacko. He's a nut, but I like his books. Or then I read Ezra Pound. He's an old, dead Russian fellow in 1920.

I stole my name and I don't mind admitting it. A long time ago, many, many years back, Jackie Gleason did a program. It used to be *Honeymooners,* and Frankie Lane used to sing "Crazy Guggenheim." It was in a bar, and right down the street was these two sisters named the Fucwha sisters. They weighed three hundred pounds. So that's part. Then I was reading, because I read a lot of books, and I found poetry. There was this guy named Dante who wrote *The Inferno,* the nine steps to hell, and I said, "I'm not going to put my feet on them steps."

So then I went to Asia, and I needed a call sign, a name. I figured, "Well, wait a minute, I knew they could not pronounce the words, so I could always be Dante Fucwha." They couldn't do it. They would mess it up, even if they went to UCLA, which a bunch of them did. So that's the name. The name came from a poet, Dante, with the steps to hell, and Fucwha, the revered three-hundred-pound sisters, just down the street from Jackie Gleason's old bar.

I still ride, but not like I used to. They cut me open, they ripped my stomach apart. I went into the hospital and I lost my stomach. I'm not physically as strong as I was to go out and do it. I think it's called "Old Folks' Boogey," when your mind makes a promise that your body can't fulfill. My brain knows what to do, my body won't do it. So I have to go slower. But I have the opportunity to pick and choose what I want to do, more so than years before. Then I would just go, 'cause going was the idea. I just went, 'cause it was there. It was fun. It was easy. Now it's physically too hard for me to do. I everything that I need, that I want, that I have to have. uld.

ɛ's nothing out there that I want to do more than riding. the utmost freedom. Take exhilaration. There's people that ʌt it immediately, and there's people that haven't got it yet. I ʮht it the very first time.

You want to do it again? You want to leave now? It might take me about twenty minutes to roll up. When a train goes by, why don't we just jump on it and go? Where? Where the train goes. I'm not dead yet.

Catching a Moving Boxcar

The typical picture of a hobo catching a train by jumping into a moving boxcar is no longer accurate. That could be done fairly easily decades ago, when boxcar floors were lower than they are now, and when the trains started up more slowly because they were pulled by steam engines. It is very difficult to get into a moving boxcar now; the floors are shoulder to head high, trains start up faster because they are pulled by diesel engines, and very few boxcars have door latches on the side of the door opening. So trainriders usually get into boxcars when they are stationary or into other kinds of cars, such as graincars, gondolas, piggybacks, or doublestacks with empty wells at the ends. Here is an account of how to catch a moving boxcar from someone who started traveling in the early 1970s, when it could be done more easily.

My mentor, Rufe, taught me how to jump boxcars by grabbing on to the door latch. On one model of boxcar there's a door latch that hangs down, like a long handle. You can grab it with both hands, always with your bare hands. You never use gloves, because gloves might slip. The door latch was always on the left side of the door opening when you're facing it. It was attached to the bulkhead, the side of the boxcar, and the remainder of the door-locking mechanism was on the door of the car itself. That part of the mechanism moved with the door, and the door latch was stationary.

When you were jumping a boxcar, you wanted to make sure it was rolling in the right direction. You couldn't hit a rolling boxcar going the wrong way, because you'd be running against the direction you'd have to swing up into the car. As you were running along the tracks, the train would be to your left, the latch would be the first thing in line, and the sliding door would be in front of you. Your left shoulder would be closest to the car.

You grab the latch handle with your left hand, then with your right hand, with your right hand lower than your left. You'd swing, and when you'd swing, you'd turn ninety degrees in the air so you'd be laying on your stomach on the floor of the boxcar. Your left shoulder would be facing the open door of the car, and your right shoulder would be facing the interior of the car. The idea was to throw your right leg and your right arm out trying to grab a depression or a crack in the floor or just a piece of rough wood or anything inside the car that would allow you to gain your balance so you could turn loose of the door latch. You're not supposed to turn loose of the door latch until you're all the way in the car.

Rufe hated hitting rolling boxcars. He didn't even like to talk about it, but he considered it to be acceptable in an extreme emergency, if you had to catch that train and there was no other way to do it. He would condemn it as thrill seeking, and he considered it to be unprofessional and dangerous. In general, his rule was that you just don't hit rolling trains unless you absolutely had no choice.

The newer model boxcars are what's called plug-door boxcars, and they have to run with the door shut. So it's impossible to ride a plug-door boxcar, because the doors aren't open.

—KABAR

The Hobo's Heart

VIRGINIA SLIM

Hoboes have plenty of time to reflect as they trudge along the tracks or sit in an empty boxcar. Virginia Slim peers beyond appearances to "quiet thoughts in longing hearts." He wandered by rail for a number of years in his twenties, but now in his late fifties has settled in Virginia.

The road never ends in the hobo's heart
But it winds and turns forever
There's no room for him in a world of men
He lives close to the wind and weather

The only roof above his head
Is a boxcar top as he rambles
It's a world of strife in a settled life
Too much to risk in a gamble

He's a happy sort as he wanders free
The backroads and railroads have known him
He has reverence for love and a God above
But no man on earth can own him

He smiles as he dreams of the long ago
When like him there were many others
The songs they sang, the stories told
Through days they spent together

And on chilly nights in the jungle camps
The warmth of the campfire sharing
Of quiet thoughts in longing hearts
Of loved ones and their caring

Of childhood days in the old homeplace
Of virtues true as mothers
Of fathers who toiled with heart and hand
Knowing other men as brothers

But his brothers are dead and he rests alone
At dusk by a rusty track
And his broken heart sings a sad refrain
Of the trains that won't come back

Of people too who rode the trains
Many places where they ran
Yet through the years and lonely nights
He goes on the best he can

The railroads are dying
His brothers are dead
Too few friendly smiles to greet him
Yet he travels on sustained by the fact
That the world could not defeat him

Frog

Frog traveled by rail for nearly thirty years before retiring from full-time hoboing, having taken his last freight ride in Montana in June 1999. He still moves around, though, and keeps in contact with those in the hobo community.

You can't get lost if you're not going anywhere in particular.   —Adman

As long as steel wheels roll, the 'bo too will roll along.   —Frog

When did I start hoboing? It depends on how you word hoboing. If you are talking about the wanderlust spirit in me, I guess when I was eight years old. If you're talking about a trainrider, railrider, it was not until 1970. I was twenty years old.

We got our first television set in 1955. I had watched television for three years, and in those three years I had seen so many different programs that I wanted to go and see and experience everything I could possibly see, everything I had seen on television. Roy Rogers, of all people, was my childhood idol; I wanted to go and be with buffaloes for a while. Then I wanted to ride horses, and I wanted to go everywhere and be with everyone and experience different places and things around the country.

When I was twenty, I was sleeping on a beach in Jacksonville, Florida. I needed to be out of there by dark, because they had a city ordinance that you couldn't sleep on the beach. I had gotten picked up, spent a night in jail, and the next day went to court. I didn't ride a train there. I had hitchhiked down there. At that time I didn't even know you could hop a freight. I had seen movies about freights, but not anything beyond that. I knew the trains were running, but I didn't know people rode trains.

I was going to head out of Jacksonville and was walking along the highway, not having any luck whatsoever getting out of town before dark by hitchhiking, and I ran into this old black man. He said, "Hey, where you headin', boy?" I said, "I just gotta get outta this town before dark." He said, "You ain't never gonna get a ride out here. I'm going to the yards and catch out. You want to catch out?" I said, "What the heck is catchin' out?" I was dumb and naïve about that stuff. And he said, "Ah, just follow me."

He went and bought two forty-pounders. A forty-pounder is a little larger than a quart bottle of beer. He got some for me because I don't drink hard liquor, and he got himself a bottle of vodka. He said, "Well, let's make our way down to the yards." And we did. I just followed him. I mean, I didn't know what the heck was going on.

We sat around in this little jungle there, and finally he said, "Our train's here. Get your stuff. We're going." I didn't have much of anything. I had a couple of blankets, but it was warm. It was summer and I was in Jacksonville, Florida, and I was headin' southwest. So it didn't matter whatsoever to me so far as the weather. I didn't know anything about getting my stuff on. I just threw it all on, including my two forty-ounce bottles of beer. It was a gondola. And he says, "You stupid fool. If those bottles are broken, you ain't having none of my vodka, because that's all you get." My two bottles of beer didn't break.

About forty, forty-five minutes later, out of the clear blue, here goes the train, it started rolling out of the yard. And oh, wow, this is nice, you're out of sight, out of mind. I wanted to play tourist, but I'm kind of scared to get up and peek around. I didn't know if I was going to get thrown off or what. We actually made it all the way into New Orleans the next day. We spent the night on the train, a night and a day.

That night as the sun was going down and the stars were coming out, as I was laying there on my blanket looking up at the sky, I felt so free of everyone and everything. This was the greatest feeling that I had ever had, and so I decided, well, this is what I want. This is what I want.

The hustle and bustle of hitchhiking would be gone from me forever from that day on. To me it was a pain in the butt to hitchhike, in that you always had to be nice. You always had to watch what you said and how you reacted to people. You had to watch out for all kinds of dangers—the drunk drivers. You never knew what kind of person was going to pick you up. It was, like I said, 1970, and there were all kinds of people just running around.

We got to New Orleans, we bailed off, and we went and got some food and grubbed up. Then we went to some kind of mission. It wasn't the Hilton, of course, but it was worth it for the grub and the shower. At that time they had these plasma centers. My partner says, "Come on, we'll go sell plasma." So we went and sold plasma and got a little road money. We really didn't want to work. The money we had from the plasma center was plenty enough.

We decided to go to Houston by freight again. We went on through, and this time we got a boxcar. This was even better, because you could sit in the center. This time I got the nerve to be touristy. I would sit close enough to the boxcar door where I could see out without being seen.

I learned a lot from this man. This went on for five years. We rode together for five years, full-time. Then he got sick. His name was Pinky. He was remembered this morning in the memorial service.

Then I was on my own pretty much. I was alone for about a year and a half, and I rode the Southern Pacific most of the way, playing yo-yo back and forth between Jacksonville, Florida, and Klamath Falls, Oregon. With Pinky it was mostly from Houston to Klamath Falls. I went back and forth and played like a yo-yo, and the same thing with my next road partner.

I made a friend with a guy named Florida Boy Blue, and we rode together for seven years. We played yo-yo for the better part of the year, just running back and forth from Jacksonville, Florida, to Klamath Falls again. We went back and forth because he was collecting his veteran's check, and he had to go back to Jacksonville, Florida, to pick up his check.

The unfortunate part of being with Blue was that we both became stone-cold winos. Well, he already was. I had never been a wine drinker until I met up with him. And then for seven straight years we lived on red port wine, pork and beans—road chili—and smoked Prince Albert tobacco. This went on for seven years just back and forth.

Our last train ride after almost seven years was a trip to Montana. We decided to expand our horizons. We went into Washington, and in Washington we're hearing all about these people running back and forth through Montana. So we decided to go to Montana and become sheep herders and do winter feedings to save sheep. That was great, we thought.

Well, we got on a train in Spokane and went, and we were totally nuts. We were so cold. We were accustomed to traveling with light gear, with warm weather gear. I froze my butt off. I jogged—the first time I ever had to jog back and forth inside of a boxcar to keep warm. My feet were just frozen solid.

But we got out to Laurel, Montana, and we immediately went down to a jungle and built as big a fire as we could to get warmed up. I told my partner, I says, "To hell with this damn sheep herding. I am going right back to Spokane or someplace where I can sell plasma or get a day's work. To heck with this crap." So we did.

That afternoon it warmed up some. It had gotten up to about fifty or sixty degrees, which was still cool. But then we had to ride all the way through Montana again to get up to Washington. It was a cold night, so we stayed huddled up in our blankets, and again we had to jog back and forth in our boxcar.

We got into Spokane the next morning, early in the morning, and then over to the shelter. It wasn't a shelter, it was just kind of a day center where you could get warmed up and have a cup of coffee. They served a couple of meals a day there, they had breakfast and lunch. So we decided that's where we wanted to stay, because we could get some work out of that shelter. And that's what we did.

We stayed there for about two months. In that two months' time my partner fell in love with this gal, and that worked out okay for them. He decided to get off the road. He wanted to get married, and that was pretty much the end of our riding together. We didn't ride at all after that. That was about twelve years ago, maybe a little more than that.

I rode by myself for quite a while after that. I think it was around 1985, or 1984, somewheres in there. Then I decided, I gotta get warmer gear. So I got warmer gear and started going back and forth through Montana. Now I was okay. I was warm enough, and I was getting to know the gist of riding both the high- and the lowline of Montana. I loved it. I didn't have to jog anymore. I had good sleeping

bags and I was staying warm and dry. And I carried a tarp. |
it was also about that time that I started carrying a tent. I wa:
young and could carry a bit more weight than I can carry no

I had one more partner after that. Along about 1986 or 19‌⌁‌, ‌oo
I would say, I met up with a guy by the name of Daniel Boone—the
very controversial FTRA president and founder. I rode with him
for five years and then was his best man at his wedding. He fell
in love, got married to a hobo woman, but I wasn't going to ride
with a couple. Her name was Boxcar Debbie. She was here at Britt
last year. They were here—well, he wasn't here, but she was here.
They've been divorced now for a number of years. Their marriage
lasted only about two or three years. It was sad, but that's the reality
of trainriders, the reality of life. If you don't get along, I guess, you
just get divorced.

I've traveled pretty much alone ever since. I choose to. But it is
inevitable that I ride with someone, because there is always somebody who wants to ride with me, so I end up riding with somebody
else, not always by choice but out of friendship reasons.

I earn money by going to day labor pools in the winter months.
In the fall, until I started coming to the hobo convention—I started
coming to the hobo convention in 1994—I used to go and pick apples
every year in September. It was a good living. I could make good
money between the pears and the apples. Then I could live for three
or four months in the United States. If I went to Mexico, I could live
for up to six months with the money that I was making.

In between jobs I always traveled by freight. I always took jobs
like in day labor places where I wasn't committed to a job, where I
didn't have to stay put in any one place for any length of time, because I got itchy feet and I just wanted to keep riding. I just wanted
to ride all the time.

What keeps me going is the wanderlust. There's always something new to see. One time I came upon a friend of mine, Dante
Fucwha, and I said, "Ah, dang it, I got on the wrong train." He says,
"You know what? You didn't. You just got to a new place, found a
new way to get to a new place." So I look upon it that way now.

I don't get tired of hoboing. Well, yah, in the last three years
I have. For the first time in my life, I had injuries sustained upon
myself from my living the life of a hobo. Some kids came up on me
and broke my leg and shattered my leg from my kneecap to my toes

and stabbed me five times in the back and left me to die on the side of the tracks as I was waiting to get on a train. Fortunately, with the three blows to the back of my head, I didn't know until I had come to that I had been stabbed and that my leg was broken. I'll always have a limp for the rest of my life. It slowed me down. As Steamtrain Maury, who is our born patriarch of hoboes, told me, "Maybe this is God's way of telling you to slow down, Frog. Slow down."

This year, though, I don't know. As king of the hoboes, it's been an immense job. Being king of the hoboes, aside from being very gratifying and rewarding, has also been very demanding on my time and on my finances. I've had to do without a whole lot of things in order to afford postage to keep up with my correspondence. I enjoy the correspondence.

Up until I sustained my injuries, I wasn't much on sitting around and writing letters to people. But, you know, in the two years since the two conventions that I've been to, '94 and '95, I was able to establish meaningful friendships with many of the old-time hoboes who had addresses, who had retired off the road, or hoboes who had addresses and were only part-time hoboing. We developed special relationships at our gatherings throughout the country in the course of the year, mainly at the convention.

Coming to the convention altered my lifestyle in that I wanted to meet up with these friends that I had made and get to know them a little bit more. In the year and the month from the time I came to the first convention, the '94 convention, I started corresponding with these people and started to develop a means and a way to allow people to get to know who I was and allow me to get to know other people.

I can't imagine myself settling down, though I would like to sometime. It's getting tougher and tougher on the rails. Every day gets harder and harder. The railroad bulls make it harder. The city police make it harder, particularly in the areas of large cities where there are many hobo jungles. They're just cleaning up the jungles, constantly cleaning up the jungles, ridding of them, bulldozing them in and over, sometimes with people's gear in there. It's awful. It's a sad reality today.

The jungles today aren't the jungles of 1970, either. I walk into a jungle today and it's like walking into a filthy dirt camp. You got to clean up everything, you got to bag up about ten bags of garbage to make it presentable enough so you can say it's a jungle. So it's changed.

I got to be called Frog this way. When I was riding freights with Florida Boy Blue, we'd go through Indio, California, quite often. We didn't have any money. In Indio, California, they stop every train and change every crew there, and it's also a checkpoint for Immigration, looking for Mexicans, illegal Mexicans, entering the country on the freight, because along the route we come to a lot of border towns. They check every train.

One day I was sleeping in the corner of a boxcar and Immigration stopped and checked inside. He says, "Any wetbacks on board?" to my partner. My partner says, "No, ain't no Mexicans, if that's what you're talking about. But my partner's name is Canadian Wetback."

They hauled me off to Immigration and interrogated me. I gave them all the information I had about myself, but I had no identification in my pocket, so they didn't believe me. My partner had all my gear, and on the third day, which was the day they would have had to release me after verifying I was an American citizen, my partner came in and told Immigration, "Oh, I found some of his identification in the bottom of his backpack. Would this work?" And they said, "Yes, it will."

So they let me go, and one of them said, "You know, we got to give him something else for a road name. Call him Frenchie or Canork or Frog or anything, anything but Canadian Wetback, because he'll get picked up if he has no identification." And my partner said, "Frog, by gosh. That sounds great. He hops on a boxcar just like a frog would, like a frog would hop on a lily pad." Florida Boy Blue said this, and the name stuck.

Unfortunately, most of my friends have a bad habit. You know how if your name is Gerard or Gerald, they'll call you Jerry, or if your name is Lawrence, they'll call you Larry? They like to add that "y" or "ie" or something. Unfortunately, my friends have the bad habit of calling me Froggie. And I've given up on telling them, "Listen, my name is Frog, not Frog-gie."

Waiting for a Train

Freight trains do not run on exact schedules as passenger trains do. They do not stop to let riders get on, and they do not always have ridable cars. So a large part of hobo life consists of waiting for trains. Here is what it is like.

Sometimes there's only one train a day. So if you miss that train, then you got the whole day to wait till the next train comes. You basically got to amuse yourself with reading or something. You're trapped. In the beginning it's not bad, but it gets to be old. You end up eating your food for that day. That's why you should always bring enough food, three to four days, because you never know when you're going to be waiting. —NEW YORK GRIZZLY

You play cards, play dice, do whatever you got to do to pass the time. It's not too bad. I never usually have to wait longer than six or seven hours for a train, maybe a night. —DIANA

I was in the Dallas yard and there weren't a lot of places to hide, because there were no woods around the yard. I was hiding in junk piles and around trains that weren't moving. I would go underneath cars and into cars to hide, and I ended up spending almost a full day and a night hiding. It was a long, hot Dallas day. The cops were real heavy, and the bulls were going back and forth. They must have been looking for something, because every train was getting checked. Finally, a train came on the other side of the train next to the one I was hiding on. I jumped up, ran underneath the train beside me, and jumped right into an open boxcar. —BUCKUP KEN

I wanted to catch a train going north. Someone who worked near the railyard I was at said that a train usually came through about three in the afternoon. No train came then. And none came that day. When it got dark, I went to a tractor trailer that was near the tracks and got in. The floor was dirty, so I spread out my cardboard and lay on it.

No trains came during the night. About 5:30 in the morning, I heard the sound of an approaching engine. I grabbed my gear, folded up the cardboard, and was out the door of the trailer in twenty seconds. The train was going slow, but not slow enough to get on. I walked after it, but it went straight through the yard, out of sight. I kept walking, and pretty soon I saw the blinking light at the end of the train. It had stopped.

I got to the train about 6:00, found an empty boxcar, and got in. The train didn't move. I slept and ate peanuts and raisins. At 11:15 I saw some yard workers nearby, so I got out with my gear and asked them whether the train was going to go north. They said that it was called for 11:20. So I got on a nearby car, a graincar, thinking the train would leave any minute. It left more than two hours later, about 1:30. Later I learned that the reason there had been no trains the previous afternoon was because of an accident down the line.

Another time I wanted to catch a train going east. I got to the yard about 7:00 or 8:00 in the evening. The last time I had been there, trains came through once every hour or two. This time none came. I found a graincar and slept on it, though not too well, because I kept listening for trains. None came.

I hung out in the yard the next day, but still no trains came. I kept hearing train whistles, though. So in the afternoon I walked west a couple of miles and discovered that the eastbound trains were heading off on some tracks that went southeast. In the evening I walked about half a mile further west, found some weeds beside the tracks, and lay down. (That got me a whole handful of chigger bites.) Eleven trains came by that night. Only two stopped. The first one that stopped did not have any ridable cars. The second one did—that was number eleven—and I got on it. It took a day and a half to catch that train. I could have done it faster if I had had my wits about me and investigated those train whistles. —ROADMAN

A Woman on the Go

CINDERBOX CINDY

*Cinderbox Cindy spent a number of her younger years on the rails.
She died in 2002 at age forty-nine. Her family scattered some of her
ashes onto nearby tracks in Texas, I scattered a few out on the rails
in northern Illinois, and the rest were buried in Britt, Iowa, at the
National Hobo Memorial during the annual memorial service there
in 2002. Preacher Steve, The Texas Madman, and I dug her grave.
The Texas Madman made her grave marker, and the three of us
lowered the marker into the dirt during the service.*

Over and over the straight folks ask me,
    "Why do you follow the life you've led?
Was it something you chose
    Or was it boredom you dread?"

They believe ladies should be content to cook and sew.
    I do those things, but I do them on the go.
I keep my home tidy and clutter-free,
    even if it is temporarily under a tree.

Housewives deal with budgets.
    Well, who can say
That I don't do the same thing
    Living day to day?

Shayla

Shayla is one of a number of younger hoboes who populate the rails. Like the older hoboes, she is unable to keep still for long. I ran into her, her dog, and her traveling companion once in Chicago. They needed a ride to a railroad yard, and I happily obliged them. They hid in bushes beside the tracks while waiting for a train, but it took them three days to catch one.

You can't ride a freight just once.
—Gypsy Moon

Hobo time doesn't mean late; it means random.
—Billy Gott

I'm nineteen, and I've always been into traveling. When I was little I used to go on road trips with my family. I had a boyfriend when I was thirteen who hopped trains, and he told me I couldn't do it because I was a girl. Then I met this guy that hopped trains. He told me that he'd take me with him the next day, and he did. He showed me what it was about and taught me how to do it and everything. We got separated and I just kept doing it. I couldn't stop.

I dropped out of high school in tenth grade. I just took off. There was a festival going on—it was summertime—and I met this guy and left with him. At first we hitchhiked a little, because I hadn't done that yet. He was putting me through the steps. Next we started hopping trains, three of us, two guys and a girl. I've been riding for a year, but I took a three-month break.

When I first started riding, it was like a dream. I was hooked right away. I'd get to a town and want to leave right away. I didn't want to stop at all for nothing. When I first stopped, when I went and took my break, it was the most horrible three months of my life. I'd hear a train's horn sometimes and I'd cry. My heart belongs to the train. I wouldn't give it up for anything. If somebody were to give me a car today and give me keys and a license and say, "You can have this just to stop riding trains," I still wouldn't do it. It's my love.

I've never traveled alone. I would do it, but I really have a fear of men, being a woman traveling by myself. There's a big risk of something happening to me. It's not a matter of I don't think I'm strong enough. I know from life as a woman that there's a lot out there to be afraid of. I get constantly hit on and followed around. I'll be somewhere, and someone will come up and offer me money to do things. It's more of a sexual thing. I don't really get disrespect in any other way than sexually. I don't think that I'm treated different as a hobo, but just as a woman.

I travel with a dog, Stazia. When I'm getting on a train, I pick her up and place her up there, and she sits and waits for me to get on. To get off, she just jumps. She can jump down but not up. I don't do it unless the train's stopped, because I don't want to risk her life.

Sometimes I get really tired of the way I'm treated. People who aren't hoboes, they'll look at me with disgust, like "What are you? Get a job. Get a life. Oh, I'll take your dog." Stupid business all the time. If you're a hobo, you're pretty much worthless as far as society goes.

What I've found is the old hoboes that are still hopping trains and stuff, they're wonderful. They have a lot of respect for anyone that's a hobo, and they're really cool. Some young ones are cool, too, but it's kind of like high school with the young ones—you're still being judged. If you want to be accepted by them, you have to wear all black. My hair wraps, I have one that's a rainbow, so I'm not a hobo. I'm an oogle, because I'm not wearing all black. That's just kid stuff. But the old hoboes are cool. I love old hoboes, they're my favorite.

I prefer sleeping outside rather than in a tent. When we go to a town, we try to find an area that's wooded or hidden. Sometimes we have to sleep in bushes in front of buildings and wake up early. We usually don't sleep if we're going to be getting on a train. We usually get off the train and go to the city and hang out there for a while and then go back. We don't usually sleep by the tracks because we got to wait for our train. We'll wait anywhere from one day to a week, depending on what's going on.

A typical day when I'm going to hop a train is, wake up, try to make money, then buy food and fill water bottles, find water bottles in dumpsters and fill them. And I gotta get it for my dog, and I gotta get dog food. That takes all day. By night I go to wherever the train is and hide out and wait for it. When there's books of maps, and you open it, I've been everywhere on the left page. Iowa and Minneapolis are the furthest east I've been.

I love gondolas, but I can't do that now because of my dog, because I have to climb a ladder with her. I really like forty-eights because you can go out on the porch. You're not supposed to—it's really dangerous—but it's like being in a convertible. You're up there and it's all air. But I got caught once, and I promised the god of trains that I wouldn't sit there again if I got away okay, which I did. So forty-eights aren't my favorite anymore, because I can't sit up there. I like grainers. I don't really like boxcars. There's a lot of room, but there's something about them—they're impersonal or something. I just don't like them.

I had a narrow escape from the train killing me. It was the first time I hopped a train after the three-month break. I was so excited because I was finally hopping a train again, and I was really anxious. It was moving, and I had to get up there in time for everyone to get on. I grabbed the ladder, and everything would have been fine, but I was watching my hands instead of my feet. There was a big metal thing on the ground—it wasn't a switch, I don't know what it was, it was a huge thing. My feet got caught on it, and it pulled me underneath the train. I looked and my legs were on the rail, my whole legs, and all I saw was the wheel coming. I thought, "Oh, no, my legs are gone." All of a sudden I was standing. My reflexes obviously threw me up. My friends said that the wheel was about a foot from me, and I did a backflip onto my feet. I don't remember doing it, I was so freaked out. I flipped up from under it and got onto my feet somehow. That was my near-death experience.

I call my mom. I'll call my dad once in a while. I pretty much don't call anybody. I'm sick of everybody. I'm just gone. My mom is pretty used to me doing drastic things, because I've lived with her my whole life, so it's not too shocking to her. She knows that there's nothing she can do about it. I'm sure she gets scared every once in a while, but she doesn't really care too much.

I've learned survival, how to be more independent. I've learned how to be stronger, not physically. You have to be strong real quick, and I've learned how to do that, because I'm kind of a weak-hearted person. I've learned that I'm capable of a lot more than I thought I was, and that I'm a lot different than what I thought I was. I've learned who I am a lot more. I see things differently now. The things that I used to think were important aren't anymore; everything of importance is completely different. I'm a lot happier.

When you're going all over the place and meeting all kinds of people, you see how they really are. If you stay in one place for a long time, you think it's just those people or something. But it's not. You learn how people really are and what society is really like. You get so sheltered when you stay in one place. And you get a lot more time to think, so you can realize what's important to you.

What keeps me going is the trains. I don't want to stop. I love it. I love the feeling of getting on a train and not knowing for sure where it's going. It doesn't scare me at all. It's exciting. It feels good to get off the train and find some random person and ask, "Where am I? What city and state is this?" They'll be like, "What?"

I can't picture myself settling down, not at this point. I can't really think about the future. I want to live my life to the fullest, and whatever that may be whenever it comes time for me to change my life, I know it'll be what I want to be doing the most, not what I need to be doing to be successful. I think if I ever settle down, it'll be getting a van or something, because I don't ever want to stop traveling. I'm going to be old and toothless and still riding the trains.

Philosophy of Hoboing

You can discover hoboes' outlook on life by listening to their poems, songs, and life stories. They take their hoboing seriously, and they value their freedom. Here are two statements reflecting these values.

I met Rufe in a train yard in Montana. He was cooking coffee on a fire beside the tracks. Back in those days, especially in the west, they didn't hassle people as much as they do now. The train workers were very unconcerned about tramps. As long as they didn't break anything or steal anything, the workers didn't care what we did.

Rufe could tell by taking one look at me that I was hungry. I was so ill-prepared that I had very little water, no decent bedroll, or anything. So he offered to feed me, and he cooked up coffee and macaroni and cheese. I was real glad to get some food. When he started talking to me, he was able to tell that it was pretty clear I didn't know what I was doing. So he started giving me an education, because I had a couple of hours before the next train came through, and he didn't want me to get on a train without knowing what to do. He started instructing me in things like slack action, not stepping on or touching the coupler, all the dangers in trying to catch a moving train, things that I knew very little about. He was trying to give me a crash education in hoboing, so that even if I was not traveling with him, I would make fewer mistakes.

I actually took off with Rufe and traveled with him for several months. I adopted his philosophy of hoboing, about tramping. His main thing was that a person should take the whole thing seriously, and he expressed that with the phrase "This ain't no hobby." This is the real deal; you should be paying attention to what you're doing. Don't be looking out the car door—you're not here on vacation. You're supposed to be riding this train as a tramp, not some wide-eyed kid who's going to wind up getting killed or injured or something.

That sort of professional attitude about riding trains, that there's a certain obligation to do things the correct way, probably reflected his own worries about what might happen to him. He didn't believe in standing up when you're riding a train. Everybody should be sitting down all the time. You never went to sleep unless you either were laying sideways against the front of the boxcar or sitting on your bindle with your back against the bulkhead and your feet toward the rear of the car.*

The other phrase that he used a lot was that he hated people who threw things down in the jungle. He'd say, "We keep a clean camp here. We ain't bums. Pick that up and put it in the fire."   —KABAR

It seems like everybody is waiting for their freedom. They're waiting until they retire so they have enough money to travel where they want to go and buy whatever they want. They're waiting until they can hop on a Harley and find their freedom on the open road. But there's only one place you can find freedom. You can't be free in the past—you either were or weren't. And you can't be free in the future—it's a myth. The only time you can be free is in this moment.

—ADMAN

*In case the train stopped suddenly.

Clearing the Yard

BO BRITT EDDIE

What is it like to ride in a boxcar out of a railroad yard? This poem tells us in vivid detail. Bo Britt Eddie experienced these details in the late 1930s and early 1940s, when he was in his late teens and early twenties. The clickity-clack is gone now because the rail joints have been replaced with ribbon rail, and the steam engines have gone to their graves, but everything else is still the same. Bo Britt Eddie died in 1997 at the age of seventy-six.

We lolled in the hillside jungle shade.
Full of coffee and stale rolls, we had it made.
We had assembled and rolled our meager pack
And watched the marshalling of boxes on a nearby yard
  track.
We smothered our coals and alerted our guard
And cautiously made our way to the railroad yard.
From the railroad ditch we spotted a well-kept box
Then crossed the bed like Reynard the fox.
We leaped aboard to a well-worn floor
Inside we checked and spiked each boxcar door.
Soon the humping stopped and a steamer brought down
They loosened the brakes, we'd soon be leaving town.
They reversed the cars all down the line
Then took up the slack and made it the first time.
Through the switches it would make a little do-si-so
That would rock the box, side and fro
Making its own distinctive sound of a clickity-click
As it made its way through every switch.
After many of these, all about the same,
And with gathering speed, we hit the main.

Now the click of the wheels on the jointed rail
Made the rhythm sound that all hoboes hail.
We sat on our packs back from a side door
We had cleared the yard, thought of the bull no more.
Out of this city into scenic countryside
We finally relaxed and hoped for a good ride.

Stretch

Like Shayla, Stretch travels with a dog. But unlike Shayla, he frequently travels alone. When his money runs out, he stops and works, but he doesn't stay too long in any one place. When he travels in winter, he puts a zero-rated down sleeping bag inside a thirty-degree-rated sleeping bag, and both of these inside a fleece liner, which keeps him a lot warmer than on his very first train ride.

Right from the first time I was hooked.
I couldn't stop doing it. It's like being a junkie
for heroin. It's hard to put roots down in a
place when you know there's that option to
go anywhere in the country.   —Drits

I beat it out of my hometown, Trenton,
New Jersey, in 1923, and ain't been back
there since. I want no part of that crowdin'.
Give me the open spaces.
                —The Hardrock Kid

Ever since I was little, I always enjoyed trains. But circumstances caused me to take my first train ride. When I was fifteen, I got kicked out of my house. I crawled into a boxcar in a local yard around my house and woke up in Albany, New York. We lived in the Boston area.

It was wintertime, it was cold, it was dark, it was noisy, and the worst thing about it was that when I woke up, the railroad employees in the yard at Albany had shut the boxcar door on me. I spent almost an hour getting it nudged open enough to where I could squeeze myself through. I would say it was probably at least below ten or twenty in that boxcar. I jogged around the boxcar two or three times, nudged the door open, a hair at a time, then jogged around the boxcar to keep warm. I didn't have a sleeping bag or anything, except for blankets, that was about it. When you go over the Berkshires in Massachusetts, it gets pretty cold in through there.

After the first trip that I made, I wanted to do it again. After four or five years of doing short trips around the New England area, I started going further away from home. By the time I was twenty-one, I was going cross-country, coast to coast. I'm thirty-one now.

I dropped out of high school when I was sixteen and ended up getting my GED later on, when I was twenty-four. Shortly after I got my GED was when I wanted to go and do my own thing. I left home permanently. I just got the wanderlust in myself and wanted to go out and see new places and enjoy the hobby that I always liked, being around railroads.

I've been around friends and family that work for the railroad, so it's not like I'm not familiar with the aspects of railroading, which helps a lot. A lot of people don't know what a wheel or a flange or a coupler is. It's things like that that help you along the road. People are getting killed out there all the time.

I've had a rule, especially because I've been traveling with a dog these last seven years—I quit catching out when the train is moving. I always catch it when it's standing still. Very seldom do I catch it on the fly. I've kept all my fingers and toes doing that.

I enjoy drinking a few beers out along the railroad tracks with friends and then going on a train ride. But I have a limit. I know when to say, "I've had enough." If I've had too much, I won't bother with the train. I'll say no.

I have never been injured, though I've been on a few trains that caught me off guard. Slack action set me for a few tumbles here and there. That's all part of the game. You should expect the unexpected sometimes.

I've woken up a few times in different places around the country being pushed over what they call the hump. That was an interesting experience, especially when you come down to the bottom of the hill and you land in the rest of the cars. The best thing to do on something like that, if you know you're going to come down, is to lay down flat with your feet facing the direction you're going. That way you won't have to worry about any head damage if you happen to go sliding. If you're at one end of the boxcar and you know that's the direction you're going, you just flip around so your feet are up against the wall. That's one of the safest ways of not getting your head bashed in.

I've always worked most places. I've always liked having money in my pocket to feed my dog and to have spending money. I quit smoking cigarettes about four years ago. I was spending about six to eight dollars a day on cigarettes. Thanks to the railroad, that quit. I did six months in the county jail for criminal trespassing. After I got out, I didn't have the craving for cigarettes anymore. The dog is the least expensive. You can buy a four-pound bag of dog food for three dollars, and it'll last him four or five days. You can feed a dog for less than a dollar a day.

I can pick up jobs anywhere, from landscaping to construction work, from shoveling snow to framing houses. It all depends on what time of the year it is, where I'm at, and the part of the country I'm in. I have friends that I can hook up with, because at most temp agencies there's no place to keep the dog, and most of them won't let you take the dog on the job site. We have a place up in Helena, Montana, that I go to a lot. It's a shelter. It's called God's Love, and they just recently finished a dog kennel up there. So I can leave him in his own little dog house and a place to run around in a field and spend the whole day working. I don't have to worry about him.

I take a little break from hoboing from time to time. Every now and then I'll get off the rails for a couple months, work, take a breather for a while, maybe do a little hitchhiking to some of the parts of the country where I can't get to by trains. I don't like to hitchhike, but it's sometimes a necessity.

I've never sat down and figured out how much I ride in a year. I know in a month's time I could usually cover two or three thousand miles, maybe more. I work for a week or a month or a couple months. It's hard to find work in some states. Employment rates can be different everywhere you go.

The only state that I haven't really explored much in this country is Michigan, because I've always bypassed it coming through Chicago going into Ohio. Never had the urge to get off. There isn't another state I haven't been to. There are some states now I've been through so much I don't have any urge to go back anymore, because of things like railroad tickets; that'll keep you away for a while.

My train name is Stretch. My mom used to call me Stretch all the time, because I was always the tallest one, between my other brother and my sister. And then my fellow trainriding friends called me Stretch because at the time I had the habit of chasing after trains. I could nab one at a pretty reasonable speed. Those days are done now.

My dog's name is Burlington. I named him Burlington because his mother almost gave birth to him on a Burlington Northern train. I knew she was pregnant. I was trying to get her into a decent lo- cation so she could have her litter of pups. I got her back home to Massachusetts, and that night she dug a big old hole in the backyard and that's where he was born. It was perfect timing. Another day and she would have had him in a boxcar.

Having a dog—it's not just for the protection. They don't ask for much, just for companionship. You treat them good, they treat you good. He's a real good watchdog. He won't let anybody come near any of my gear. I can leave him tied to my backpack and nobody'd steal it. They'd have to shoot him to steal it.

Things haven't really changed much on the rails, except that they are getting a bit tougher to ride nowadays because all the rail- roads are merging together and security is tightening down. I've started switching over to some of the short lines, smaller railroads. They're a little more lenient on trespassers. Some of them, they'll actually put you on a train. Stay out of sight, that's all they ask. I'm real careful. I haven't been in jail in seven years, since I've had a dog. Because if I go to jail, my dog goes to jail, and after a certain amount of time they'll put him to sleep.

I've run into all different kinds of people, some good, some bad. You just gotta know how to judge somebody. You can tell after a while, is this the fellow you want to hang out with or is he gonna wait till you turn your back and stab you in the throat or something. It's all a matter of how you take care of yourself. After many years on the rails, you get a reputation.

It's a small world out there. Everybody knows everybody. Somebody does something to somebody, it's going to come around real quick, and that person'll be found fairly quick. What happens then depends on who it is. It's more of a family kind of thing. If somebody stole my dog out there on the rails, I could put a pretty good bet on it that seventy-five percent of my friends would be looking for that dog. And they'd get him back for me. Word will get around not fast fast, but it will spread fairly quick. One person will run into another person down the road; things just kind of come together sooner or later.

I've associated with all the good, all the bad hoboes. They haven't done nothing to harm me, so I have nothing bad to say about them. Sometimes somebody might do something stupid. That happens, you know. As far as all the murders and stuff that are going on, a lot of it is the kids that are out there that cause the problems. The old trainriders that have been out many years, they're the ones that know better. Now you got these new kids who are calling themselves the new FTRA. They're the ones out there robbing people, killing people, stuff like that. It's changed in the last ten years. Even when I first started coming out long-distance, it wasn't that bad. I don't know too many of them. I just stay to myself most of the time. But I know most of the old-timers. A lot of the old-timers, they're getting off the rails, slowly, little by little, natural causes. We've lost a lot of the old family, old age or heart problems.

About two years ago, I was in a yard, and a bunch of us, about eight of us, were walking along this train looking for a ride, because we knew it was getting ready to pull. Somebody had previously walked the train and knew there was an open boxcar about three-quarters of the way down the train, which was a pretty good walk. When you walk a train, you always want to keep other rides open in case he starts to pull quick. Well, I forgot to do that. I'm looking down there, there's the open boxcar ten cars down, and he starts to pull out of the yard. I look forward, and the only thing I remember seeing was two grainers three cars back. So it was either the boxcar ten cars down, which I couldn't a got, or those grainers.

I ran back three cars. By that time he was starting to move along. I was able to get Burlington on the train, my pack, my water jug, my grub sack. I was running along and I jumped on the ladder, but I didn't have the energy to pull myself up. So I rested my kneecaps on the ladder and just hung there rolling through the yard. I finally got the energy to pull myself up, barely. And after I went through all that work, they stopped to throw a switch. I cried. Then after the train got out of town a little ways, they stopped in the hole to let another train go by. I walked on down to the open boxcars. That was about the closest thing I ever—the craziest thing I ever did.

I play one day at a time. I try to figure out what direction I want to go, where I want to go next. Sometimes I just play Russian roulette. I will see an old boxcar, get on it, take it where it goes. That's a new thing. Little by little you realize you're running out of places to go. I've been to practically all the major division points. That's why I've started doing some of these short line railroads and some lines I've never rid before.

I've tried settling down a few times. Last winter I was down in Arizona, and I had a construction framing job for three months, ten dollars an hour job. I had my own apartment and everything. I just had that itch in me; it bothered me for almost a week. Then I dropped everything. I left the job, I left the apartment, I left the keys in the door, the deposit and all. I just picked up my backpack and went. I even left a brand new nineteen-inch color TV behind. It's things like that that you sacrifice. It's hard. Once you get it in your blood, it's there. It's not going to go away.

Arrested

Many hoboes have been arrested and sent to jail, sometimes for a day, sometimes for thirty days. For hoboes, though, being in jail is a cause not for shame or guilt, but for annoyance. It is an irritating interruption, an unwanted intrusion, as these accounts illustrate.

I was riding a freight toward Cheyenne. They told me way back down the line, I guess in Lincoln, Nebraska, "There's a certain sign as you go into town, the first sign, a big billboard sign. You get off at it." I was laying on the train, sleeping, and I found myself going into town. I thought, "Uh-oh, I better get up and look for that sign." I didn't see it. Got off. Started walking over to the highway and saw a guy looking like an ordinary fellow, dressed ordinary, common dress, walking toward me. I thought, "I'm going to try to speed it up and get over to the road."

I didn't quite make it. He walked up to me and said, "I'm so and so. Who are you?" I told him who I was. He said, "Where're you going?" I said, "I'm heading out to California." By the time he had his hand on his gun, he said, "I'm the railroad police. You're under arrest. Get in that car over there, and don't try to run." He told me, "Don't ever let me or any of the other railroad police catch you on the Union Pacific." That scared me to death. I didn't ride a Union Pacific for three or four years.

I spent three weeks in the county jail in Cheyenne, eating beans. I didn't like it too well, being in jail. It took my freedom away.

—HOBO CHARLIE

I spent a month in jail this last March or April. I didn't even get caught on the train. There were six of us; we ran through the woods after the train broke up in the yard, and the bull caught us on the other side of the woods and arrested us. I was in jail for a month. It felt stupid. I didn't feel like I did anything wrong. I wasn't hurting anybody. It would be one thing if I was robbing the trains and breaking into the containers and stealing stuff, but I wasn't doing anything illegal. I was just riding the train. I guess that's the way the ball bounces. Everybody has got to do their time.   —DIANA

Shanty by the Main

IOWA BLACKIE

*Hoboes sleep (kip) where they can—under bridges, on trains, in
cemeteries, back in the woods. It is especially nice to find a little shack.
Iowa Blackie, who has traveled for more than thirty years, mostly
in Iowa, probably knows where dozens of them are in that state. I
drove him to one once. We walked to an abandoned shed at the edge
of a railroad yard, he put his stuff inside, and I bid him a friendly
"See you down the road." Blackie has written several books of poetry,
which he sells wherever he goes.*

Not much this shanty near the main
Four cobbled walls and single door
Some boarded over window panes
A wooden bench and bare wood floor

Sufficient though in case of rain
A temporary place to kip
While waiting for an outbound train
An interlude on lengthy trips

Hobo Monikers

Hoboes leave their monikers on bridges, train cars, and anywhere else it suits them. This one by Stretch was drawn on a bridge in Minnesota, and the one by the artistic Shortstop was drawn on a boxcar in Pennsylvania. They may still be there. Adman took these photos of them.

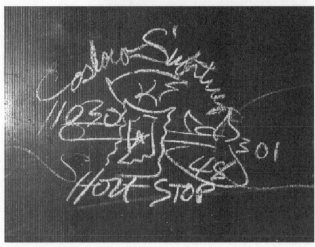

Shortstop

Shortstop quit art school when he was nineteen in order to travel, which he did for about four years. In addition to working at numerous jobs, he sold his art and other crafts in order to support himself. Last year he took to the sea for some months, then slept on the docks when he returned. Someone noticed his artwork there, and now he lives in California, where he uses his artistic talent in a variety of jobs. The drawing that follows his story is one that he produced and sold while traveling on the rails. He cut out an 18" x 24" stencil, placed it on light blue or white paperboard of the same size, then spray painted over the stencil, and sold the resulting drawings for ten dollars each.

> I wouldn't trade anything for what I learned on the road. You understand human nature so much better.
> —The Pennsylvania Kid

> I can go coast to coast on a piece of toast.
> —Connecticut Slim

What got me interested in riding trains was the neighborhood I grew up in. It was in Kokomo, Indiana, with steel mills all around me. There was a camp not too far down the tracks from where I lived, and occasionally there'd be a couple old guys that would come in. Every once in a while, me and neighborhood kids would sneak down there and talk to those guys. They'd tell us stories. We'd jump on the sides of the trains and ride them as far as we could until they'd stop it. The guys in the caboose would usually come out, and they'd throw us off every time. We were just on the ladder, but it was dangerous. I'm surprised nobody got hurt. I was in the third grade at the time. There were older kids that could make it all the way across the trestle. We didn't ever make it that far.

As I got older, I worked construction with my grandpa. He hired drifters and occasionally hoboes that rode the trains. I talked to those guys. A couple of them told me stories about trains. I'd always made artwork, I've always been an artist, and I won a full-ride scholarship to an art school in Baltimore at the Art Institute of Maryland. I went there for close to a year. But I didn't agree with the school. I didn't agree with the politics of it. I came from a different neighborhood than other kids there.

The old B & O track went right through there, CSX now, and I would watch those trains every single day. I decided I was going to get on one. I didn't know anything about riding trains at all. I didn't have any gear. All I had with me when I took my first ride was a pretty thick sweatshirt. I had no blanket, no food, no water, nothing. I got on, and within about two minutes of being on the train, not even that, I was in a tunnel underneath Baltimore city.

The tunnel is four or five miles long, and it goes up a grade. It was never built properly; the ventilation system has never been right in that tunnel. I've read history books on it. So the diesel smoke picked up real thick in that tunnel, and I didn't think I was going to make it out. I didn't know anything about breathing through a rag or pouring water on it. I didn't have any water to pour on. I was riding the head end of a graincar. I thought I was going to pass out, because that tunnel really picks up gas. Anyway, I made it through the tunnel, barely. I made it into Washington, D.C., and took public transportation back the next day. I camped out in a trash dumpster to keep warm, because it was almost wintertime and I didn't have anything. The sweatshirt wasn't enough.

I dropped out of school two days later. This was my first year of school. I told the president of the school I didn't want any part of it. He says, "Well, you don't have to pay a dime to go here." He says, "Now why in the world would you want to drop out?" I said, "I'm going to drop out and I'm going to ride trains." He thought that was ridiculous. But I walked out, and I've never regretted it. I was nineteen, almost twenty. It was 1997. I'm twenty-three, almost twenty-four, now. I've been riding probably about three years, a little over. Full-time, mainly.

I know a lot of kids are out there three hundred and sixty-five days a year on trains. I was never like that. I would go ride for eight hours to the next town, because in the east you don't get these huge, long rides a lot of times. I'd get junk trains. I'd find work, sometimes work for a week, sometimes work for two days, go to the next place. If I had a little bit of money, I'd find another way out. Didn't always ride the train, but I rode the train quite a bit. I rode all through Indiana, the old Wabash line in between Detroit and St. Louis. And I got to know all those towns real well.

I fed alligators in Kansas City. I fed them raw chicken—had to hit them in the face with a raw chicken on a stick until they ate it. Lady has them in a backyard there. She's got, I think, twenty-six alligators. Most of them are full-size. She lives down around Truce Street in Kansas City. She just does it on her own.

It was me and my buddy, traveling together, and farming alligators in Kansas City. We ended up getting thrown out of Kansas City, kind of. We were in Westport, and a guy was beating on his wife. He started kicking his dog in the face, so I took some mace and I sprayed him down with it. I figured that nobody else was taking care of this guy, so I took care of him. The police got ahold of me. They knew I was in the right—they had a history with this guy. But they told us to be gone by morning. So we got out of there and went to Denver.

I did a lot of construction work. There was all kinds of different jobs. I ran a forklift. I worked for the railroad. I've worked in a glass factory. I've worked in scrap metal yards. I helped picked oranges. I've cleaned people's refrigerators, busted out sidewalks, done yard work, all kinds of work. Any little thing I could get I would do. When I couldn't find work, I started making artwork. I developed a printing press I could use out on the road. I would do it by cutting out a posterboard and then spray painting it.

I'd do work for the labor unions for free. I'd donate it to the IWW—the Industrial Workers of the World—which I joined up with in Baltimore. After that I started selling stuff out on the road. I would do wood carvings out of fruit crates and cigar boxes. I'd carve out notches, layer it up, and make secret slide compartments. Then I'd sell those on the street. I could get twenty dollars out of them. I'd carve people's names in nickels for fifty cents. I still do that. In Vegas I was making nickels that say "Good Luck." I'd sell those for a dollar on Fremont Street there.

Anything I could do for money besides panhandling, I'll do. I don't panhandle. I've never found too much of a need for it because I can always find a job, or make my own job if I can't find one, and make twice as much money and still have some integrity out of what I do.

I've never stayed in a mission. I've always stayed beside the railroad tracks. Sometimes I meet nice people in towns who will let me stay on their back porch for a night or stay inside, even. I make friends in towns because I've been going around to so many different towns. They're happy to see me when I come back. Now I don't have to sleep outside as much anymore.

A railroad yard in Indiana gave me and another guy a boxcar to live in. That's where I got my road name at, from an old tramp named Birddog that as far as I know is still living in that boxcar. He's an old-timer, he rode for a lot of years, and he's settling off. He's settling off so that he can die. He doesn't want to be out anymore. He gave me my name because I'd stop through and I'd never stay. I'd stop in and never tell him I was going. I'd just be gone and be back again in three months. So he told me he wanted me to tell him when I was going because he didn't know where I'd be. That's how I got my name. Called me Shortstop.

I don't know what keeps me going. I've really wanted to stop now. I want to stop and settle down. It's getting harder to ride. In the east it's not as practical to ride as it is to hitchhike. And even that's getting hard. You got to deal with a lot of train yards out there, because your divisions are closer together. It's more than I like to deal with. I been finding good work lately—eighteen-dollar-an-hour jobs in construction. I started carrying a tool belt around with me, because I found I'd get better work. So now I'm thinking maybe I'll settle down in Chicago. For a long time what kept me going was being on the train. I love that feeling.

To me there's nothing better than riding a train at nighttime, a night train, going through the backyards of every town and seeing the honest side of people. In the front yards, when you're driving a car, they've got it all tidied up. In the backyards, they've got their stuff that makes them who they are. Sometimes you can watch them in their windows as you go by. A lot of East Coast towns, they're right by the tracks. Smelling clothes on the clothes line. You smell laundry detergent when you've been around nothing but grease and rust. I love the feeling of being on the train, ninety thousand tons of steel going sixty miles per hour. There's nothing else like it.

I rode through a derailment recently. It wasn't my train that derailed. I was going past another train that had derailed, apparently a couple of weeks beforehand. They hadn't gotten the mess cleaned up, though. Coming out of a town in Indiana, the boxcar I was in started shaking all around. I didn't know what was going on. I looked out the door, and there was railcars scattered all down the embankment. Trees snapped off. There was one boxcar sticking out of the river right underneath the trestle. The rails we were going on were warped or something, so the boxcar was really shaking me around. I thought my train was going to leave the track. It was shaking all over the place.

I get tired of hoboing when I'm waiting on a train. You have to wait for twelve, fifteen hours, or two days, and the mosquitoes are getting you. It ain't worth it. You can get to the next town hitchhiking easier. You can find another way. I get tired of it all the time. But then when I stop, I look back at it. I'll say, "Man, sleeping in the rain that night wasn't all that bad. I'll go back out and do that again."

I've had a girlfriend for five years on the East Coast. I've been with her steady all through the time I been on the road. She's been patient. I'm afraid that patience is gonna wear thin. I don't want to lose that. I meet a lot of guys that may not have had that chance. I got the ability to make artwork and have a way out. And I think I'm going to take advantage of that. I probably still will always ride occasionally. But I don't want to live on the road. It's getting old.

I've traveled mainly from Baltimore down to Louisville. I've been to every single state, not all of it by rail. I haven't been to Maine. I haven't been to Alaska or Hawaii. Most of my railriding has been done east of the Mississippi—Indiana, Illinois, Ohio, and into Baltimore. I never really rode into the south, because I have no desire to go south. I been down to all those states, but in the east there's better jobs. In the west it seems harder to find construction jobs. People underbid you. In the east you can find pretty good work, because the buildings are older and they're falling apart more. That's my theory on it—old brick buildings—you can get jobs tuckpointing the bricks, patching roofs—the old hot roofs—there's a million jobs out there.

I like to work. I don't like to work for nothing. But I like to go to a town and build something and then go back and say, "I built that.

I helped on that." I like that feeling. I've had some nice jobs. I've had some good bosses, and I've had some really bad bosses at carnivals that never did me good. I'll never work the carnival again.

There's a lot more security out there now. The thing is that now it's not always the bull that'll get you. It's people. In the East Coast, it's congested. Rail lines go by a lot of highways, so you'll be right there along the road, and people'll see you. They got cell phones and they'll call in. I got caught and thrown in jail over that once. The engineer came back and threw rocks at me. I was on a graincar. The train had stopped, went in the hole. I just thought it was waiting on a train to go by. I didn't think anything of it. All of sudden I hear rocks shuffling, and a ballast rock comes and hits the porch of my graincar. So I'm thinking there's kids out there throwing rocks. I get up and look, and it's the engineer. He says, "Get off the train."

I got off the train. I got my stuff. My buddy was with me, because we rode together for a little while. The engineer comes back and says, "What are you doing on my train?" I say, "We're just trying to get where we need to go. We don't mean to hold you up." He says, "You're holding up the whole railroad." I said, "We didn't ask you to stop. That's your own choice to stop." I said, "We'll get off your train if that's what you want." He says, "We got the state police and the sheriff coming out after you guys. You better hide."

So we took off—tried to hide in a wheat field. We waited there for a couple of hours. We thought the coast would be clear. We went and got on the highway to hitchhike out. Soon as we got out there the sheriff came, asked us if we were the two guys who got caught on the train. I says, "No, we weren't on no train." We both said no. He looked at my tattoos, sees a boxcar and some other stuff, and he goes, "You mean to tell me you guys weren't on a train? We got the report." I said, "No, we weren't on that train." He says, "I'll find out real quick." I looked at my buddy and say, "Yeah, we were on it. We didn't intend for it to stop here."

They actually treated us real nice. Put us in jail for two days. Ended up the warden gave us birthday cake because it was her birthday. She wanted to hear our stories about the trains. They treated us real nice in jail. I was surprised. The judge didn't treat us so nice. Got probation for one year, nonreporting, two-hundred-and-fifty-dollar fine, and if we were ever caught in the state of Indiana on another train, it was thirty days in jail. Things like that make it kind of not worth it. When you get tickets in your home state, you got to pay them. I don't want a warrant out in my home state. I can't go visit my family. So I had to pay it. That made me think a bit.

A typical day? It depends on what I'm doing. If I got a job, I work it. If it's good, I enjoy it. It's better than hanging out on the main drag. That gets old. That's why I work half the time. I don't want to sit down all day on the sidewalk. When I do that, it's boring. It's so boring, your day feels like it's a week long. You feel like your day never ends. But if I got a job, it goes by quicker. I don't drink alcohol or do any drugs, so I don't have fun that-a-way. I go out and take walks down the tracks, look for things on the ground, look for things I can make stuff out of. Just enjoy the land where I'm at.

Once my buddy and I were trying to get out of a yard in Baltimore. He goes and tries to get a boxcar while it's moving. He didn't know anything about getting the latch. Puts his elbows up on the floor. He's a skinny guy, doesn't have any muscle at all to him. I was coming up behind him, and I grab him off the thing. I was afraid he was going to go under. I don't know if he would have, I just grabbed him off it.

I almost got my leg caught in the wheel of a graincar. That scared me. It was icy on the rungs of the ladder. My foot slipped through the bottom rung and barely touched the wheel. Man, that made me think. I didn't like that much. I'm scared to death when I see the wheels on the track.

I used to carry only a blanket, a wool military blanket, with a sleeping bag in the middle. I'd carry about two or three cans of canned food, usually some beans or some other type of soup, a couple of road flares. I would heat up the soup with the road flare. You can't leave those on for long, those things are hot. I carry a change of clothes, a pair of nice clothes so I can dress up and be somewhat clean, and a pair of dark clothes so I can't be seen. Gloves, water, not a whole lot. Now I carry a tent. I got a frame pack. As soon as I got that, I started carrying a bunch of useless stuff that I really don't need. It's easier on my shoulder. It feels nice. It helps you out when you have to walk a huge stretch, when you get put off in the middle of nowhere. It was nice having just a bedroll, though, because it was only fifteen or twenty pounds.

One thing I learned real quick was that I didn't really have an appreciation for this country before I hit the tracks, before I seen it by rail. I was in the bottoms of everything—living outside, working low-wage jobs, getting beat out of my pay, learning what capitalism really was, instead of just reading it in a book.

I got beat out of a week of work in the carnival. I got paid twenty-five dollars. Another time I worked in a tube in a steel yard. I'd say it was thirty-five feet high. I had to climb up on a ladder inside the tube. This was in the middle of summer. The tube was about three feet in diameter—it wasn't much room. They give me a pickaxe with no handle and a shovel with no handle, no respirator. I had to go in and clean out the steel that had got clogged up in this tube while the sun was baking down on it. It was like on oven. I had to push the stuff down the other end of the tube into a chopper. You fall down into the chopper, it spits you out into the pile. This was through a day labor organization.

I worked for about seven hours on that job, and I quit. I came out so black, it was all in my mouth like I'd been in a coal mine. It was all over me, everywhere. I had metal shavings embedded under my skin. I got paid—my paycheck was five dollars and sixty-five cents. I went into the day labor office. I said, "There must be some kind of mistake." They said, "We took out money for your hard hat." There was no way I could bite it. I didn't know what to do about it. I don't work for day labor anymore. I don't believe in day labor. I don't believe in taking a job that a man fed his kids with and giving it to any joker that walks through the door, paying him a day's wage. I won't do it unless I'm starving. I can find a million other things to do than day labor

I rode a boxcar once and forgot to block the door. I actually didn't think that I needed to block the door. I was doing a short run and I thought, "Ah, no big deal," because oftentimes the doors are so jammed shut, it doesn't seem like it matters. But this time the door moved. I had cardboard that I had found in the boxcar—there was a lot of it—so I folded it up and blocked it in the track of the door, so it wouldn't go all the way shut. By the time I got to where I was going, I was scared.

I never have gotten hurt. I feel safer on a train than in a car. You get to hitchhiking with people, and drunks pick you up. I learned you can tell the personality of a person by the way they drive their car sometimes. Within the first twenty miles, if they're a tailgater, you know they're probably some kind of pushy person.

I stick to myself. I had a guy in a yard out east want to ride with me. He had no bedroll, nothing. He had a jean jacket—this was wintertime—and he wanted to go to Maryland with me. He was real into going with me for some reason, and he was a wino. I didn't trust that guy. I had some gear, and I knew he was eyeing it up. I run into very few people out there, very few. There's not a lot of people who regularly ride out east, not like there is in the west.

I try to get on trains when they're stopped if I can. One thing I learned by my old hobo friend in Indiana, he rode during the Depression—he dove off of a train. I don't know what yard he was in. He was trying to beat some bull there, and he dove in the dark and hit a switch dolly, and it cleaved half of his face in. So at nighttime I shine my light instead of just jumping off. I try to jump off when it is going as slow as possible. I don't like to go into the yard. I jump off before the yard. I don't want to deal with that.

My family's not so happy that I quit a full-ride college education to become a hobo. They don't come right out and say it, not anymore, not to me, but I know that they don't like it at all. They think I could be doing a lot more with myself than what I'm doing.

I keep in touch with my grandparents. I left home when I was fifteen. Never really went back too much after that. I wanted to see bigger, better places. I traveled a lot before I ever went to art school—never by trains, though, just by getting rides from friends, ending up in different states.

I could be doing better with myself, I guess. But I've had a good time and I don't regret it. It's been hard. I've learned a lot more on the rails and living on the road than I ever learned in a year of art school, or than I could ever learn in any school. I've learned things that couldn't be taught by a book, things you just have to learn by living in it, things you come to understand about yourself by being alone for long periods of time. It's been an important experience to me. Even if I stopped, it's changed the way I see the whole world forever.

Drawing by Shortstop

In the Jungle

During the Depression, hobo jungles were a common sight. They were located near bridges or rivers and were populated by large numbers of job seekers trying to survive. Now they have nearly disappeared, and only a handful of travelers frequent them. They have also changed, as these accounts indicate.

I've been in lots of jungles all over the country, from California up through the northern states down through the southern states. They didn't have fancy chairs, but maybe an old stump that they'd drug up to sit on, maybe a brick, a few old milk crates, or a little five-gallon bucket turned upside down. A lot of the guys just laid around the camp and talked, sitting around a pot of beans or some kind of stew. —HOBO CHARLIE

A hobo stew is different from other stews, because, one, it was cooked outside, two, everyone contributed to the ingredients, and three, it's good, especially along with a little wine. As people come along to eat the stew, the charge was one item contributed to the pot.

—JAMES FREELS

Things have changed. I remember days when you'd get off the train at night and see a fire and yell at it, "Hello, fire!" Whoever's there would yell back, "Yeah, come on" if they're awake, and invite you in. If you didn't have a cigarette, they'd give you one and a cup of coffee. They'd give you a meal, because tomorrow when you got up, you'd go make your hustle, and when you came back, you'd offer them back what they gave you. Nowadays, the society among the tramps is different. The camaraderie doesn't seem the same like it used to be. —NOMAD

The jungles that I saw in Montana and other places when I first started riding were very unelaborate. Many of them were nothing more than just a spot that was cleared out in a grove of trees or somewhere close to the tracks. There weren't any tables or chairs or anything like that. And most of the time there wasn't even a source of water, although the best jungles that we stayed in did have a water faucet somewhere close by or somewhere to get some water.

The jungles I see now are very trash-strewn. They're not more elaborate, but they often have something like old furniture in the jungle, and it's kind of all wet and nasty. I see a lot of beer cans and stuff like that thrown on the ground. I see a lot of broken glass in the jungle, which is something that would never have been tolerated when I was a kid. As a matter of fact, the guy that taught me how to tramp, Rufe, almost got in a fight with somebody one time because he broke a bottle in the camp. It wasn't so much that people walk around barefoot, but it was just the idea that it was disrespectful to do something like that. Throwing trash on the ground in front of other tramps in the jungle was almost like a provocation to fight.

One time a guy got up when we were sitting around a fire in the jungle—it was in Washington State—and walked about ten feet from the camp, unzipped his pants, and began urinating. All the older guys were really angry. They got up and started like they were going to attack him in a group. It was considered to be more than just unhygienic. It was like, "This is our home, and what is wrong with you? You don't have any respect for us, and you don't have any respect for yourself that you would do something so thoughtless. Being drunk is no excuse. You shouldn't drink so much that you lose the ability to discern between what is appropriate and what is not appropriate." That was a big violation of the rules, to relieve yourself anywhere close to the camp.   —KABAR

Sitting Around Our Little Fires

OKLAHOMA SLIM

Hoboes are like everyone else in many ways: some are genuine and some pretend, some are honest and some dissemble. Oklahoma Slim, who traveled for a number of years during the Depression, was not afraid to tell the truth about life. He died in 1999. The drawing is by Drummond Mansfield.

We sat around
our little fires
smoking Bull Durham
and drinking
coffee
dreaming
scheming
lying
about the fish we'd caught
the money we'd made
the whiskey we'd drunk
the women we'd had
we was lonely
we was losers
and we knew it
but wouldn't face it.

B

B traveled for several years in his early twenties after graduating from a university in New York City. He put his university training in acting to good use on the road by doing performances in various places. His political views have led him to Australia, where he travels with a political action group.

Play the hand that is dealt you.
    —from the grave marker of Oklahoma Slim

For a gypsy, it's not what you're on when you're moving, it's how you move when you're on it.
                                       —B

How did I start hoboing? I never had been around railroad yards or anything. When I was eighteen, I had a dream about riding a freight train and I thought it would be a neat adventure, so I talked to my best friend in high school at the time. The next year we finally got around to doing it. We did a short run—a one-hundred-and-fifty-mile run—from New York City to Albany, New York, and didn't know a drop of what we were doing. We caught a boxcar on the fly, about seven miles per hour. I had a big old backpack with a tent and a hibachi grill, things you just don't need, and we waved to every single car and passing train on the way out, thinking it was like a parade.

When we got there, the cops were waiting for us. We jumped off the boxcar, smiling, so excited. The cop ID'd us, put us into his car, and started driving us out of the yard. As he did so, he called in to his dispatcher and told him that we had escaped. Then he told us that he was going to drive us to the downtown area. My friend's immediate response was, "How am I going to get out of the city? We're going to take a bus back." But I was trying to remember every left and right turn he was making so I could figure out how to get back to the yard.

I didn't know anybody else rode trains, so it was hard to find someone else to ride with. I didn't associate it with any sort of life-style. It was just an adventurous thing, doing trips for fun. But now freight train riding has a lot of different resonances for me than when I first started.

I went to Fordham University, Lincoln Center, where I was a performance arts major, and I graduated when I was twenty-one—that was three years ago. I guess I was your secure, average college liberal with no sense of reflecting that in my daily life, except that I rode trains, which was just about adventure. I didn't associate it then with any political ideology.

I graduated at the top of my class, and I was cast in an off-Broadway show, an adaptation of *Faustus*. It was supposed to start in two months, but the funding fell through and the whole thing went abust. I just assumed—I was a little arrogant kid, a bit preten-tious—"Well, I'll take my freight-hopping skill and combine it with my performance skill, and I'll create a show that'll tour across the country on freight trains, and people will be so amazed that it will be my slingshot into climbing the ladder in the industry." So I adapted an Ibsen play—*Peer Gynt*—me and a friend, a woman. It was a very, very low-tech adaptation. We did a premier in New York, and we traveled to Cleveland. We did the show there at coffeehouses and stuff. We traveled by freight train, all by freight, just us.

We made it to Chicago, still not really associated with any po-litical people, just doing the summer run. We were setting up the show in Chicago, staying at a hostel, and we met another traveling performer who was a clown. He hitchhiked mostly, and he just fol-lowed the sun. The clown and the woman I was traveling with fell in love. So we tried to work him into the show with us. But instead she decided to become a clown, and they left and went to Canada together for a clown festival.

At that point I didn't know what to do, because the show was written for two people. My whole world collapsed—everything, all the promise that was expected of me. I was devastated, so I caught a freight out to La Crosse. It was intimidating. I was still young and hadn't met any other tramps who had ridden trains. For the most part it was me convincing my friends to do it. And those are the worst people to travel with, because if they don't naturally like it, you're trying to impose these experiences.

I made it to Britt and met Lee. After the convention I traveled with him and David and a man named Harvey; we all did a trip out to the West Coast to see Lee's forest squatting. He pretty much cracked my head open. He was the first person to challenge the world that I had known. Being an anarchist and just a beautiful person, he challenged the background that I came from.

We would pass by a beautiful mountain of trees, and Lee would point out that those trees weren't native to the area. Being from New York City, I thought it was beautiful as it was, but I realized that it had been manipulated by man, that it really was a chimera. And I also saw all the land that had been grazed, the flatlands, the dried-up lands that had been dammed, the environmental impact.

We traveled pretty hard, so there were the resonances of traveling with Lee and also getting harassed by police and waking up to a dog and two cops with nine-millimeter guns on me in a freight train yard and realizing that the world is not what I expected it to be. I learned that you cannot work from within to change the world, that change happens slowly, if at all, and that it takes people to be outside of it to present the ideas of change to people who are willing to adopt them and change the world from within.

I got back to New York with a schizophrenia. Now all of a sudden there was this thing revealed to me that I couldn't very well turn back on, and it created all kinds of crazy emotional responses in me that I had a hard time negotiating. So I cracked, and I wanted to be on the road again.

The crack produced a lot of things. I went to explore the political community that up until that time had been mysterious and stand-offish to me. I didn't know anything about the anarchist community or the politically active community or the squatter community. The people on the Lower East Side in New York City who had info shops of challenging literature and who were taking over abandoned buildings and renovating them for practical housing—I wanted to be part of that, because it felt so much more like a direct connection to real people. So my life veered drastically. I realized that my life had to look a lot like the work I was doing, and if it didn't, then I wasn't worth anything.

Riding freight trains became for me more about taking money away from the transportation industry that was fueling the world that I was willing to throw out the window, an industry that was not about being supportive or caring. Basically I felt that freight train hopping was a class issue, except for some joyrider with a scanner. But even they don't realize that they are vicariously living through people who have chosen to participate in a life of poverty, a life of stealing rides on freight trains, of trespassing, of fourth-degree misdemeanors, of potentially doing time in jail.

You cannot make that a cool experience. There is nothing fun about being processed through the system. When a cop sees you, poor and homeless, they're going to treat you like that. All the world you left behind is irrelevant at that point. You feel not a part of this world. You learn very quickly that this country is not as free as it professes to be. Freight train hopping for me is really about that, about people who are disenfranchised emotionally, spiritually, physically, ideologically, politically, finding the last place to be free. And mainstream culture, I think, has a hard time dealing with it.

Freight train riding is a big part of my life, but not the overriding part. Depending on where I am and what I'm doing, I'm either an actor or a squatter or a train rider or a community organizer. At this point it's pretty much the only way I get around besides hitchhiking, just because of the pure beauty of riding trains. It's absolutely magnificent. And also the cost—you can't beat it.

In the five years I've been hopping freights, I have seventeen thousand miles logged, which isn't a lot for a full-time rider, but it's nothing to sneeze at, either. It's been in most of the states. I've missed Louisiana, so far, and Alaska and Hawaii. Maybe South Dakota, too.

What happens in traveling is that it is really difficult to find a way to sustain it. When you've been recharged and you're going to jump onto the freight train, you have a lot of energy. But it quickly gets depleted with the responsibility of taking care of yourself. After a while, even being in relationship with people is very draining. The world doesn't see what you're doing as a valid exchange for what they're giving you. People don't realize that by your being out on the highway shaking hands with somebody, that is like a job. I need to be out there doing that, because otherwise I would lose connections with others.

So I'm trying to combat the tiring aspect by finding ways to do my creative work while traveling. In that way I have a sense of integrity about traveling. It's a valid alternative lifestyle, not just some sort of reaction to how bad the world is or to coming from a bad home. I'm very much nomadic. I really love meeting new people, having new experiences, and visiting new places.

What keeps me going more than anything else is other people who do this as well, who are different ages, different sexes, different colors than me, who I have a kinship with. I'm not alone out there. Other people out there are also enjoying the benefits of this lifestyle. That validates it for me.

To earn money, at first I would do street performing, whatever I could do, in various cities. Other times I would just travel, then crash and go back to some sedentary world for a little bit. I haven't paid rent in three years, so I have not had an apartment in three years. I squat, stay with friends, whatever. I've got some electrical skills that I fall back on. I would hit the road again with a little bit of money and then crash—tired and broke. It takes too much work to get food. You need to go somewhere to recuperate.

Recently I was unloading trucks with day labor organizations. That was really degrading, because you get six dollars an hour and they take out all these little tiny sucker fees, like for the gloves you have to wear and the bell which they require. So you only get five dollars an hour. You bust your butt all day long, and you walk out with thirty-eight dollars.

Most recently I've been living off my other work, my performing. Basically I've been making enough money to survive on just performing. That feels so good. I'm not making a lot of money by any means. I walk out of each city with between a hundred and fifty and two hundred dollars. I'm also falling back on a lot of other things. I'm still dumpster-diving for my food and stuff like that. But it all works out. I'm surviving pretty comfortably. I don't have any worries right now, and I've got enough money in my pocket to save for little things.

There's others out there, too, who are finding ways to sustain themselves with art ideas about the world. We want to find a way to survive and exercise our creative impulse and still feel like valid human beings. So we're trying to get our resources together and support each other.

How many shirts do I have? This is the only one. Pairs of pants? This is the only one. Pairs of socks? Three. You need socks.

I've had different ideas about settling down over these years, and where I'm at now is I'm combining an old idea with a new idea.

I hope someday to have a place, a house, which I build, where that is my base. I'll probably spend a few months out of the year at this house, and I'll know that whenever I'm road-weary or need a place to do my work, a place to spread my ideas out on the table and create a new project, I can go there. I'm also hoping that in the traveling I do—say, for example, I go on a tour for six months—I'm hoping that through other people I know we can create a community where I can offer my house to someone else for the time I'm not there.

I still feel very strongly about spending a lot of time in transit, sharing the work. What I do is create performances. The only way I feel they work is if I share them with as many different people as possible. That is where the rewards of the work come from.

I don't know where the house is going to be. Right now I'm asking questions about this country. In America, every city tends to look a lot the same. We've got the same stores, the same perspectives, even. We're all buying the same mitts and have the same fears. Trying to find diversity in this country has become more and more difficult.

Over the winter I tramped out to Arizona to see my family, and I crossed the border into Mexico. What I was struck by was the kids, the children, how their eyes had such soul in them. It's a different life. I think the life we live defines us, and I'm somehow missing a soulful connection with America and the people in it. I find really beautiful people, but they're scattered all around the country, and it's hard to feel that we are evolving in a positive direction with everything that's happening.

There's a bankruptcy of soul right now in America. So I want to go overseas for a little while and see if there's another place where I can spend my short little time on earth in peace. I can still do my work—be a tourist throughout the world and hopefully America, and share my work that way.

I didn't have stories in my life before I traveled, and now I have stories. I guess the best thing is the insane spirituality that arises out of traveling—surrendering everything that you're supposed to be and surviving, not having much money and seeing how things come to you. I'm not a religious person, but I can see spiritual things that are happening to me.

When people have extended themselves or when you say, "I really wish I had a coat," bam! one would come. It just comes to you. If you surrender your trust into relaxing that things will be okay, things will be okay. What you need will come to you. As long as you trust, have faith, it will come. The more faith you have, the more of a rhythm that's established, the more things come. And the more scared you get and start to grasp and think, "I've got to get money, I've got to do this job," something bad is going to happen. The more that happens, the less things come to you.

I don't have any religion, though. My concept of God is that I see God in other people. I believe God is no bigger than other people. Everyone dies, and I don't define things any more than I can.

I don't have a typical day. Recently, most of my days are spent architecting how my performance stuff is going to be sustainable, how I'm going to do it and adhere to what I believe. I want no part of any industry. I want to do this traveling around, by freight, by hitch-hiking, and find whoever I can as an audience. The other things I'm doing are just sitting and thinking about ways to make it better.

I'm a bit worried about the future. I get worried that I'm going to fall in love with somebody and it's going to compromise some-how this way of living. I'm not really willing to compromise what I've learned, because it's much bigger than me. Hopefully I can find a partner who would be willing to see that and would want to do it for themselves. That's the only way. But I'm scared, because I've worked so hard to get where I'm at and to feel comfortable and proud of myself. Finally, after these five years of hopping, I'm starting to find a way to have pride.

Photos

CLOCKWISE FROM TOP:
OKLAHOMA SLIM,
CINDERBOX CINDY,
OATS,
NOMAD,
IOWA BLACKIE.

A Hobo Story

THE TEXAS MADMAN

Hoboes like a good story as much as the rest of us do. The author of the following story, whose life story is included in this book, will look you straight in the eye and declare that it is a hundred percent true—nothing made up, nothing added, and nothing left out, either.

The Northbound

In July of 1994 I stopped at La Crosse, Wisconsin, to pick some blackberries, knowing that I could sell them to local restaurants to drum up some traveling money. After my three-day stay, I walked to Grand Crossing, where the Milwaukee Road crosses the Great Northern. This is the usual spot where I catch out north to Minneapolis. It's usual for rail fans to park here and watch or photograph passing trains. As I was waiting for a northbound train to come in, a man of about sixty years approached me and began talking to me. He turned out to be a retired Great Northern conductor, and he unfolded an interesting story that would become even more real to me that very same night.

It seems that a hobo used to travel in and out of La Crosse picking apples during various seasons in the forties and fifties. One year the hobo came upon a newly born Great Dane puppy in the weeds, whining, malnourished, and scared. The hobo adopted this dog, as did the dog the hobo. These two traveled in and out of La Crosse by train many times during the next several years. The hobo had taught the dog to sit at the end of a string of cars while he went to look over the train for a ride.

After finding the car he wanted to ride on, the hobo would give a shout. The dog, hearing his master's voice, would come trotting down the train and jump in the car that the hobo was sitting in. For many years the two of them traveled in and out of La Crosse this way.

Then came a time when the hobo had to leave town and travel to St. Paul on urgent family business. As usual the Great Dane was sitting at the end of a train waiting for the hobo to whistle or shout. This particular day a northbound and southbound were sitting side by side. The hobo shouted for his dog to come. The dog came trotting down the tracks, but before he could reach his master, both trains began to pull. The hobo began to shout louder now, but the Great Dane, confused in all the noise, jumped on the wrong train. And from that time, for the next three years, the hobo and his companion were separated. Employees for Great Northern in La Crosse would often see the hobo travel into town looking for his dog, only to jump the next train out, missing the Great Dane, who had come to town on a later train looking for his master.

Then came the day that a northbound and a southbound pulled in side by side, the hobo on one train and the dog on the other. Man and beast were finally reunited, and never a more grand and happy reunion than this has ever been seen. Afterwards, the hobo and the dog caught a northbound train, never to be seen again.

The Great Northern conductor paused for a minute, and I waited anxiously to hear the rest of the story. "Ya know, when hoboes die they call it catching the westbound, but this hobo and his dog caught the northbound. Every night, from the last week of July to the first week of August, a ghost train rolls north on this line. An old steam engine pulls a rattling string of boxcars, and if you watch closely, on one car will be a man smiling and waving and a big dog looking out and barking."

Well about the time he finished his story, my train came in. So I said my goodbyes and boarded. I sailed along on the train in the dark, cool night. At midnight, it pulled into a passing track. Then I heard it, the old moaning of a steam whistle, the chug-chug-chug of a steam engine, and the rattling of an empty string of cars. Soon it all was passing me. And on one boxcar was a man smiling and waving, with a big dog looking out and barking. As God is my witness, that old hobo and his dog really did catch the northbound!

The Hobo and His Bedroll

BO BRITT EDDIE

*This poem makes readers feel as if they are actually watching a
hobo get his bedroll together. For Bo Britt Eddie, the routine was
once a daily occurrence. He wrote numerous poems describing his
experiences, another of which is included earlier in this book.*

The hobo arose from the dampened ground
And rubbed his eyes as he gazed around.
He smoothed his tattered clothes with a grimy hand
And looked about in this newfound land.
In a trash-strewn jungle beside the railroad track
He scrutinized it good 'cause he'd probably never be back.
He picked his soiled bedroll off the lumpy dirt
And observed the earth that made his body hurt.
He took a piece of canvas from the bedroll pack;
On the earth he again laid it down and back.
He folded the edges and smoothed it out
And again surveyed the area as he looked about.
Next came a much-holed blanket to its place
Upon the canvas properly, he was in no haste.
Then came the tattered rags from years of yore.
He smoothed them down and patted it all some more.
Then came the wrappings and newspapers of days gone by
Which he pressed out as he watched the threatening sky.
He again adjusted the edges and folded them in;
Not to do it all properly was a hobo's sin.

He rolled his pack as he humbly thanked the Lord
And wrapped and tied this roll with a dirty cord.
He placed, then adjusted, this roll to his back
And made his way to the nearby railroad track.
He walked to a railway siding against the wind.
As the way-freight entered, he was on the road again.

Preacher Steve

Like many hoboes, Preacher Steve has slowed down after many years on the rails. In 2000, when he was forty-nine, he married Half Track in hobo fashion—at a jungle fire with fellow hoboes for witnesses. Grandpa Dudley, who performed the ceremony, had them throw the bitter part of rhubarb into the fire—the leaves—and keep the sweet part—the stalks—as a symbol of their life together. After pronouncing them married, the hobo witnesses surrounded the two with congratulations. They are staying put for the time being.

A true blue American hobo is someone who has knocked on back doors asking for work for a bite to eat, been bit by dogs, been in lots of jails and missions, and who is also the railroad's most famous nonpaying passenger.
—Rambling Rudy, a hobo from 1925 to 1932

I always had this thing that I wanted to go places. Even when I was a little kid, like two years old, my mom used to tell me, when they took us on family vacations, I'd be sleeping and I'd wake up and ask if we were going home. They'd say "No," I was fine, but they'd say "Yes," I started crying.

I grew up in a small town, in Oskaloosa, Iowa, south of Des Moines. The hoboes used to come to my grandmother's place. One of the first hoboes I ever met was Fry Pan Jack. I met him off the tracks in Oskaloosa.

By the time I was thirteen or fourteen, it was okay for me to hitchhike. I had friends all across the state. So my mom let me hitchhike around, which was nice. Then we moved out to Rochester, New

York, in 1964, when I was still in high school. I worked for Eastman Kodak for a little while, but had to leave when I was nineteen. That was in 1970.

I decided to go out to Denver and Colorado. I hitchhiked out there and got some day labor. It was the middle of winter, and the day labor was running out. This person said, "I know how we can catch a train down to Kansas City. There's a lot of work down there." So all right, I'm game. I've never been on a train before in my life. So I get on the train with him. This is the dead of winter—no bedroll, no nothing. We go through an ice storm in Kansas. But we made it. Actually, I took a half-pint of whisky with me. Back in those days, I drank a lot of scotch and whisky. And that half-pint lasted me all the way. I was doing jumping jacks and everything else in that boxcar trying to keep warm. That pint of whisky almost froze, it was that cold at times.

It got in my blood then. I figured, man, this is a lot easier than hitchhiking. I rode for a while, tried to settle down. I was twenty-one then. That was 1971. Almost everyplace I went, I'd go work day labor, or else I would stop other places. For a while there I had places where I could go in for a week or two and work, because people would be on vacation. I did a lot of construction out in the Washington, D.C., area. Every time I called and told them I was going to be coming back through, I had a job for as long as I wanted. It was for a day or three weeks or something like that.

It gets in your blood when you start riding. And once it's in there, it's hard to break. I stopped a couple times and got full-time jobs, but they didn't last long. The longest one lasted a little over a year. It was good money I was making, but it was just time to go. In '84 I ran into Dante Fucwha. We hit it off, and Dante and I started traveling together. We rode year in and year out. Sometimes we'd ride out to Spokane, Washington, from Minneapolis three times a month. Dante and I put in probably three-quarters of a million miles riding together for fifteen years. I'd been riding before that, so I would say I've got a million miles on the road.

Sometimes we rode when it was fifty below. It's the gear you carry. You can't go out with us if you don't have the gear. We're not going to let anybody freeze to death on us. We're going to go out when it's cold because we know what we need out there. We've been there.

Your water jug. Don't fill it all the way up. If you fill it all the way up in the winter, it's going to freeze. You got a better chance for it if it's only partway full, because it will shake. And when it's shaking, the water won't freeze as fast as it will if it's completely full. If it's full, there's no air in there. There's no nothing, so the water can't move when it shakes.

You take either a twelve-pack with you or you have a newspaper or something with you so that you can start a fire. Fusies are always great. You carry empty bread bags to put your dirty socks in so that they don't get in your other things. You change socks any time they get wet. You can always dry them. Because if your feet get wet, you're going to die. You carry a warm blanket in your tarp, and extra down—a sleeping bag—for the cold. Gloves, you carry good winter gloves. You don't go out there with nothing. You can die within ten, fifteen minutes just walking in weather like that.

I was in Minot, North Dakota, when it was actually fifty below, and they couldn't do the wind-chill. We were all warm underneath, but the police came down and told us we had to put out the fire. We were going to freeze to death, they said. I said, "Why are you waking me up to tell me I'm going to freeze to death when I got all this stuff on?" But they told us we had to put out the fire because it was too cold to ride. They told us to go hitchhike. That didn't make no sense to me, because it was easier staying underneath the bridge, with the fire, waiting for our train, than it was to go out and hitchhike when we got to be out in the wind. They drove us out to the truck stop and a couple guys tried to hitchhike, but I just went back down and caught a train.

What kept me going those years was the people I knew, and the freedom. After a while when you're out there, you meet people all across the country. You'd be surprised at the people you meet and the friendships you make. And then you got to go back and see them. If there's one way to get back there, you know how to get back there. So then you go and you get your jobs lined up so you can afford to do it. There's so many old people that you haven't seen in fifteen years, maybe twenty years. Some people stay in a certain area when they ride, but once in a while they stray out. You can't run into them until they go back to that area. But when you run into them, that's just great.

I've tried to stop a couple of times and have full-time jobs, but all of a sudden I get itchy feet. When that train whistle blows, by the fourth or fifth time it blows, hey, it's about time I get up and go. Throw up your stuff, here comes that train, it's time.

It's the freedom, the stars, the scenery, the new people I was able to meet, the new places to see. I've seen so much across the United States that nobody has ever seen before. You go riding across the highline, and maybe you're on a grainer and you're going up the hills of Montana and you're coming out of Helena or going by Kalispell, and, look, over there, there's a great big mama doe with her little fawn, and she's nursing it under a shade tree. You see things like that.

You see the Great Tetons, you see the Grand Canyon, and you get to see them from a perspective that other people can never see them from, because the tracks go where the roads don't go. You can't see this stuff on a tour or a bus. It's just beautiful. I mean, it's great. You get on an open boxcar. How many people carry a ninety-inch screen with them? When you open up that boxcar door and look out, you got the screen, and there's no commercials or reruns. If it's nice, you open up both sides, and then you get to see out both sides.

I was a mason, but I haven't done it for years. That's the reason why I can always go back and work in the Washington, D.C., area. I can do it in other places, too. I did it down in Tulsa. A lot of it was day labor, so I was able to pick up a lot of that. I worked for the Cedar Rapids *Gazette* as a pressman for the newspaper. I trained a lot of other foremans, because we had the new Goss offset. When other big newspapers got it, they'd send their foremans in for a week to work with us to see how it would run. And I was the supervisor for a warehouse. That didn't last too long, either, because it was time to go. It was good money, but the money don't mean that much out here. It really doesn't. You just say, I don't care. It's time to go.

I tell you what. I used to be able to make it from Spokane, Washington, to Minneapolis with a package of tobacco, a jug of water, and a can of beans. If I wanted some beer, then I would need a little extra money. Other than that, you don't need that much. You can go a long ways with a little bit of money.

One time I was in charge of eight stores in Lafayette, and I ended up in McDonald's on maintenance. But that lasted less than a year. I was doing the hiring for their maintenance people for their other stores. I was like a supervisor in that one area for the maintenance people. Then that didn't matter. And the other jobs—you might have to dig a ditch, but that's okay. You be hungry, you can dig a ditch. What's wrong with digging a ditch? I mean, someone's got to do it.

Everybody gets tired of hoboing once in awhile. I got tired of it lately because of stuff that's been going on with the tracks. It's been getting harder, and I'm getting older. You get out there, and you're so sick at times that all you can do is crawl underneath someplace and almost pray to God that you're dying, because you're that sick. You're laid up for two or three days like that and you're by yourself—that can be tiring. If you look back, you can count it as a blessing. Yet when you're out there twenty-four hours a day for a few years, it can get tiring. But doesn't anything get tiring after a while? You can get tired of watching TV. You can get tired of listening to a radio. You can get tired of your own job once in a while even though it's your career. You get tired of it, but you don't quit it. You realize you're tired and that's okay. Maybe you take a break. When you work you get vacations, so maybe once in a while you stop someplace and take a break from riding. A lot of people do this.

It's harder to ride now because you got people out there that don't respect things. When I was first riding, we used to have jungles all over the United States. You could leave your pots and pans in these places. You could hang them from trees. The grills would be there for you. There'd be firewood there for you. There'd be everything. We would have little hooches all over. Our jungles would be all right. They were always left there, and there was always a can of food or something in there. So if you came in out of a pouring-down rain or out of a snowstorm or something, there was something there. At least you could get your fire and get warmed. The only thing anybody ever asked was, before you leave, replace it if you can. If you came in and you had something extra, an extra can of food or something, you left it there anyhow.

Then they started coming in and wanted to burn down the hooches for the wood instead of going out and getting their own. You got more violence out there than we had before. The bulls are getting tougher. They're getting more restrictions on us if we get caught. It's worth it to do it once in a while, but it's not worth it for me to be out there all the rest of my life now that I'm this age. I'm fifty-two now.

Once I was riding with some people—it was in 1987, I think—and we wanted to go through a certain area at a certain time of night. We had already been through it in the morning and were showing these people this area. We were pulling into Havre, Montana, and we needed tobacco and cold beer. It was a hundred degrees out. So I said, "I'll just jump off here. You guys go on," because where we were on the train, I was going to have to walk a mile and a half back anyhow. So I jumped off and slipped on the rocks wrong.

I was with another good trainrider, Dante Fucwha, and he knew right away something was wrong. He says to the others, "Steve just did something. I'm getting off and go back and see what happened," because he saw I wasn't getting off right. It looked like I was, but then afterwards I started to stagger a little bit. He goes, "This doesn't look right."

What happened was that I lost the toes on my left foot. The train ran over them. I was lucky I didn't go completely under because of the way I hit the rocks. Actually the train just barely got my toes; it didn't cut any of them off. They just had to be cut off afterwards. If you look at my shoes, you'll see where they head up at the toes. I don't have anything in there but socks. They wanted to give me a prosthetic and special shoes, but that costs money. So, no, I just put socks in there. It didn't stop me from riding. Just as soon as I got through with it, I started riding again. I had been out there for almost twenty years at the time.

I got called Preacher Steve when I was doing the maintenance thing in Wichita, Kansas. At the time, my boss was a minister, so on Sundays we used to go to halfway houses where the people couldn't go to church, group homes where they couldn't get out. We'd take the gospel message to them during the afternoon on Sundays. When people found that out, they started calling me Preacher Steve, which was good, because then a lot of people would come up to me on the tracks and ask me what I thought something in the Bible meant. I would give them my interpretation. Once you get a name, a lot of times it sticks. You can give yourself your own name, but that don't work if someone else gives you another name and it goes around. "Preacher Steve" stuck.

You know, everybody always said I rode alone. Well, I've never rode alone in my life. I don't walk alone. Everyplace I go, there's someone with me. Jesus is always there with me. Everyplace I go,

Jesus is there with me. Even if I should happen to go in a bar and sin, he is still with me. He might be tapping my shoulder and saying, "Hey." He's that silent footstep right next to me. I'm a sinner and I know it, but he's always there with me.

A typical day means getting up, rolling up my bedroll if I'm planning on moving that day, or if I'm jungled up, then I go get some firewood, water, and food. If I'm riding, then it's rolling up, getting on the tracks, waiting for the train, and jumping it. I probably already got my water and everything with me. It's just getting on and riding for maybe another thousand miles until I want to get off. That's pretty much it.

I'm not going to get on without my water, I'm not going to get on without my food. I'm probably not going to get on without my tobacco. I can without my beer, but other than that, that's about all I need to roll off. If you're in the jungle, you got to go out and get your food, you got to have your firewood, you got to have your water—anything that you feel that is important to you to have. If you want pop, you have your pop. Whatever you carry extra, you carry it.

So that's a typical day. You just go out and wait by the side of the tracks. Maybe you have a book or something to read while you're sitting there looking at the track. When the train pulls in, well, good.

I was riding with somebody one day, it was Dante, and we weren't in too big of a hurry. We'd been enjoying ourselves; we'd been taking a little break for a couple of days, and we're getting bored. So we decided it's time to ride. We walk up and sit down, and here comes the train. We're looking it over, and we see an open boxcar down by the bridge we'd been under. Naaah, there'll be another one. If the open boxcar don't pull up right here, we ain't getting on it. We were comfortable. Guess what pulled up right in front of us? An open boxcar. I guess this is our ride. We only had thirty feet to walk to jump on it.

I've learned to respect that train a lot. I've learned a lot of tolerance. I've learned a lot of patience. A lot of patience. You can't be in a hurry. You have to have patience. You got to be able to live with yourself, because if you can't live with yourself, you're not going to make it out there. A lot of times I travel by myself, and you might be sitting out there for twelve, fifteen, eighteen hours waiting for a train, or two days, depending on where you're at. If you can't live with yourself, you're not going to make it.

You need tolerance with other people if they're riding with you, tolerance with your own self, even. Gratitude. Work ethics, because you have to work. And you can be humbled, because it doesn't matter what you're going to do. If you're to dig a ditch or something, that's okay to do that. Even if it's pulling weeds, it's okay to do it. You're not bumming, you're not begging. You're doing something for your money. Plus closer to myself and closer to God. And accepting things as they come. Taking the weather as it is, because it doesn't do any good to complain about it. If there's something you can change, then maybe you want to change it. If there isn't, just accept it, because you can't change it. You just accept people as they are, until they prove different.

Good Turns

Hobo living is rough. You get wet and cold and debilitated by the heat. You get hungry and thirsty, and your clothes get dirty. The constant drain on your energy wears you out. Now and then, however, something nice happens. Every hobo has a story like one of these.

I was about five miles from the yard, and I'm really, really hot. I'm walking along, and a postal worker in one of those postal trucks picked me up. He stopped and he goes, "Do you need a ride?" I say, "Yeah, I could use a ride." He says, "Where're you going?" I say, "Down to the yard." So he opens up the back of the mail thing, and all this mail's in there, and he says, "Just throw your pack in there. I hope you don't mind, it's going to get dark when I shut the thing." I say, "No problem." He drives me five miles to the yard. He pulls right up to the train I got to get on. I grab my backpack, climb up into the gondola, I'm on the train, and boom, it goes.

—NEW YORK GRIZZLY

I had just gotten off a freight train up in Billings, Montana. It had started to drizzle, so I said, "I'm not going to sleep in this graincar and be out in the open all night." I found a loading dock and lay down my tarp with my bedroll on top of it. "At least I'll get out of the rain," I thought. I woke up in the morning, and it's pouring rain and snowing to boot. I said, "Well, at least I got two bucks in my pocket. I can go dry my sleeping bag and have a cup of coffee. A buck might dry my sleeping bag, it might not, but it'll get me dry enough to get back on the train to get on to Helena," which was my final destination.

I got off the loading dock, rolled up my sleeping bag as tight as I can, as wet as it was, and started walking down the street. There's a motel across the street, and a man yells at me, "Sir, are you homeless?" I say, "Some people say I am. I just got off a freight train, and I'm headed to a place to get my stuff dried." He says, "Come here."

So I go over, and he goes inside the motel office. I say, "I'll just wait out here for him. I don't know what this guy is, if he's dealing or if he's going to bring me a cup of coffee or pastry or what."

He comes back out and he says, "No, sir, come in, come in. I want you to fill out a registration card." I say, "Sir, I have no money to buy a motel room. I only have money to dry my sleeping bag and get a cup of coffee." He says, "Come on in, fill out this registration card. It's already taken care of, somebody took care of it."

I go on in and start filling out the registration card, and he says, "Would you like a cup of coffee?" "Yes," I say. Then he asks, "How do you like it? Black?" "Yes," I say. He brings the coffee over and sets it down. I finish signing the registration card and turn around to say thank you, and he's gone. I say to the clerk, "What happened to that man? I have no money. How am I going to pay for this?" He says, "It's been taken care of. Here's your key, and here's an envelope he left for you."

I walk away. I'm curious and I feel like something is wrong, but I don't know what. I go to the room and look inside the envelope, and there's a hundred dollar bill in there. And I say, "This is the day I met Jesus. This is the day I met Jesus."   —FROG

Making a Nighttime Run

THE TEXAS MADMAN

Whether you ride during the day or night, the rails sing and the wind blows. If you are an authentic hobo, you will experience a melding with the train. "It's just you and the train," The Texas Madman once remarked. Riding freight trains is not just fun; it is life. This poem was written in Grand Junction, Colorado, after its author crossed the Tennessee Pass on the Rio Grande Railroad in 1989.

Making a nighttime run,
the mainline is oh so clear,
with no more red block lights,
or other trains to hear.

The rails are singing loud,
the wheels, they love to whine,
the wind in my face is crisp and clear,
it's me, the train, and time.

Don't care which line I'm riding,
don't care which way I go,
the nighttime is clear, stars shining,
it makes my greasy blood flow.

For some, night riding is old hat,
for me it's always fun,
to exercise my freedom,
to make a nighttime run.

New York Grizzly

New York Grizzly credits train riding with keeping him alive. He had given up on life, but found himself with an irresistible urge to move, which he satisfied by traveling on the rails. That urge, though strong for nearly fifteen years, has been replaced with a desire to make a life in the company of others who stay put. He now lives in an apartment in a small city in the west.

It is a lonesome journey in an empty boxcar.
—Jeff Davis

When the going gets tough, all one has to do is get one foot in front of the other.
—Road Hog

I started hoboing in 1986 when I was twenty-three. I've been out here thirteen, fourteen years. Everybody has their own reasons for being out here. I sort of gave up on life, so mine is not like everybody else's. I went to college for police, and I was in the military. The last job I had I was a correctional officer for the State of Pennsylvania. I worked out of New York City, New Jersey, and Philadelphia with kids that killed other kids and stuff. After about eight months of that, I gave up on life. I just stressed out. I walked away from everything, and literally I'm out on the street.

Basically, I took life into simple forms, air, water, food, and shelter. Air is free, water is semi-free, shelter is a piece of plastic, and food is from a dumpster or wherever you can get it.

My first train ride was in Tucson, Arizona. I was sitting outside a park close to the Salvation Army. I had no money. I had gotten tired of hitchhiking, because of the weirdos out there. The train comes by, probably around thirteen, fourteen miles an hour. I knew nothing about trains. I used to play with them as a kid, but I knew nothing about catching a train. I knew I wanted to get out of there, because I didn't like the heat and I was hungry and living on the street. I just wanted to get out of there. So I grabbed ahold of the train.

When you first start riding trains and you don't know what you're doing, you don't think that you're supposed to run to keep up with the train before you grab it. So what I did is I grabbed without first running with the train, and I felt a burning sensation in my arm. Then I'm running along the train, but I wouldn't let go and it was dragging me. I finally let go, and I hit the dirt and got cut.

This old hobo, I don't know who he was, comes up to me and says, "Son, come here, I have to talk to you." He pulled me aside and he goes, "There's three things you need to know." I was young, and I wasn't about to listen to some old man. But I did listen to him because of the burning sensation that was still going on in my arm. He said, "If you can't count the lug nuts on the train, then don't catch it." He goes, "If there's one unit, then it means it's going into the yard. If there's three units, it's going distance. When you grab ahold of the ladder on the train, lift your feet up; pick your feet up when you grab it." The next train came by about an hour later. It comes smokin' through there, and I grabbed ahold of that thing and did everything he said, and it worked. I got on the train.

It was a grainer and it had grain in it. It was a hundred and fifteen degrees. I had a gallon and a half of water when I got on, and I went all the way to Phoenix. By the time I got to Phoenix, I had about half an inch of water left in both jugs. That was it, total. I went right in the yard, didn't even think about the railroad police or anything like that. The guy comes up to me in his white truck. He rolls down his tinted windows, he looks at me and he shakes his head, he rolls up his windows and drives away. I'm sitting there, saying, "What's going on here?" Then I say, "I got to get out of here," because it's pretty bad there. They throw you in jail, even back then.

So I go beelining for the gate. Just before I get to the gate, another guy pulls up, rolls down his window, looks at me, shakes his head, and drives away. Now I'm curious. I get off the railroad property, and I'm breathing good now, knowing that I'm not going to go to jail. I find the next gas station, and I go inside the restroom.

What happened was, with the hundred-and-fifteen-degree heat, I sweated so much that the grain—somehow it was white grain—went all over my face, and I looked like a monster. That explained why they just shook their heads and drove away. It was like, "This guy had a bad enough time as it is." Really, I had a very enjoyable ride. But to their eyes, looking at me, it looked like I had a bad day.

The work I do varies. For the first seven years, it was pretty bad. I was working here, working there, anywhere to make a buck. Sometimes it was hard making a buck. For those seven years, I ate out of food banks, missions, food stamps, dumpsters.

Food banks back then were actually very good. Now they're not good at all. You used to be able to get two big bags of groceries when you went to a food bank back in that era, but now you get—they call them transit bags. It's a sandwich, a thing of beanie weenies, enough to get you to the next town, and God help you if the train breaks down. You're going to have a bad day. But even though it was good back then, it wasn't that good.

After seven years, I got my disability. I needed it. It saved my life, actually, because I was getting pretty torn up. The road can tear you up. It can tear you up after years and years of being on it. But I just cut off my disability, because I want nothing to do with the government. Right now, I run the sign. I hold the sign up, "Hungry, Veteran, Broke, Need Food, Money." I do quite well at it. And I dig in dumpsters for food, items, anything I can sell, anything valuable that can get me money so I can eat.

Generally I don't drink. I drink a couple times a year when I'm around my brothers and we're in friendship. It's all happy stuff. It ain't none of the negative stuff.

I get called New York Grizzly because I carry grizzly bear mace with me and I'm from Adirondack, New York. Grizzly bear mace shoots thirty feet. I can knock five guys down at thirty feet with it. It's pepper spray. I like to be called New York Griz or just Griz.

What keeps me going is God. I love God. God protects me from evil and gives me the wisdom to counteract evil, and He also gives me the wisdom to deal with people so that I know who I'm supposed to talk to or not. There's a lot of nice people out here, and there's a lot of cockaroaches. Those are the bad people with no morals, no con- science, no nothing. And I'm the biggest can of Raid they seen.

God guides me everywhere I go. There's been trains that I've hopped on, if I would've took the first one, I would've died. There was a derail on it. And this has happened numerous, numerous, numerous times. I believe everything happens for a reason.

I don't know what drives me. I have to keep moving. I feel compelled to do that, and I don't know why. But I'm slowing down. After all these years, I'm slowing down. Not my riding, I'm just slowing down inside. I think it's because I got rid of lot of my anger. When I first came out here, I was a very angry person. I was dealing with stuff that happened to me in the military and stuff that I had seen when I was a correctional officer. I gave up.

The trains, I give them credit, because they have actually kept me alive. I would have been dead years ago if it wasn't for them. I have to keep moving all the time. It's not uncommon for me to be in eighteen, twenty states a month. I move like the wind.

I know what I want. I want to get married and have kids. I want to be happy. I don't want to be rich. I can picture myself settling down in my mind, but in reality, I don't know. I don't know if I have the strength to deal with the responsibilities. I have a hard time sleeping in a bed, I've been sleeping outside so many years.

I sleep in the weeds next to the tracks, usually near the yard. I'm addicted to trains. I'm addicted to the sounds. I feel very comfortable around the brakemen and the yard people. There's just that feeling. It's a safety zone. In the yards nobody goes usually.

And the bulls, actually, I have friends, bulls that are my friends, all over the United States. Yes. These guys, I feel safe around them. It's nice to know that when you wake up in the morning, a yard worker will come by and smile and know you're camping out next to his yard. I'll go have coffee with them. There's a lot of places in the United States where I've actually had coffee with these guys when I come into town. That's why I have such a good patch collection, because they came from them. Over the years you build up a rapport with them.

I hate to be violent, but unfortunately, if you're not on top of things, then things happen to you. You got to understand that when you're in every major city in the United States, sometimes you have to be aggressive. Sometimes you can't put your tail between your legs and run. You have to stand up to these people.

I get problems all the time, not on the rails, but you got home guards, you got mission stiffs, you got street people, you got a whole lot of different people who are always trying to get into your game or rob you or take your gear or this and that. And I'm a one-man person, so I have to be ready for everything. I travel alone, mostly, but I have access to my brothers any time I need them. It's just a matter of getting in touch with them.

A typical day for me is up early in the morning. I get on the train, I eat breakfast—I always eat breakfast. And I usually don't cook it; I usually go into McDonald's, Hardee's, or anyplace. I have a lot of friends in a lot of places throughout the United States. I just eat there, and they know me when I go through their town. This is where I eat and where I shop, at their store.

It varies, too. Some days I get depressed and I'll hide. I'll go into a storm sewer and I'll hide for four days. I won't see nobody. I don't want to see nobody, don't want to talk to nobody, just want everybody to leave me alone. Some days I'm more open and I'm willing to talk to you, but then there's other days I would never talk to you. You couldn't forklift me to talk to you. I just want to be left alone.

One big thing that really bothers me is that they have a stigma of a hobo that you got to be dirty. You can't be clean. You can't be clean-cut to be a hobo or ride the rails or be a tramp. I think that's wrong, because I keep myself clean. I take a shower, I cut my hair, I shave, and I do stuff like that.

There's a lot to know out here, and we suffer sometimes. I have to get out of my bedroll every day. It's warm, toasty, in that bedroll. When you get out of that thing when it's snowing and it's subzero, you're going to freeze. On the highline when it is below zero, you have to sleep with your water, you have to sleep with your food, because if you don't it will freeze.

I usually sleep on the ground. I never sleep underneath bridges. I'd rather pull a piece of plastic over the top of me. Many times I do that in the wintertime, because I don't want to unload all my stuff out of my pack. So what I'll do is put cardboard over top and then I'll wake up, push the snow off, and pull up the bag.

I usually carry a tent with me. I had a tent that blew away and stuck into a tree in Bellingham, Washington. It was a fifty-mile-an-hour wind, and it stuck into a pine tree. When it hit the wood, it went ssccrrreeee, and the tree destroyed it. Seconds. It blew and it stuck right into the branch.

Traveling for me is easy all the way around, because I'm pretty stealthy. I went to college for police, and I was also in the military, so I'm always on top of things. But it is harder, too, because the laws are changing. When I first came out here, it was trespassing. Now it's criminal trespassing, which is a misdemeanor. Trespassing is just a violation. Now they also have a law called theft of services, which is a free ride, which is also classified as a misdemeanor.

I got stopped in Idaho. The bull told me, "I can get you for criminal trespassing, which is a misdemeanor, which is thirty days in jail." And he goes, "And I can get you for theft of services, which is a free ride, which is thirty days in jail. I can also get you for littering, which is thirty days in jail, and that's another misdemeanor. But I'm not, so get out of here." He let me go, but he didn't have to. This is what I could have got. Ninety days. So it's a pretty serious thing. That's taking ninety days out of my life.

I have to keep moving all the time, so for somebody to lock me up for ninety days might put me over the edge. When you're dealing with air, water, food, and shelter, stuff like that, you basically are just trying to survive. When people toy with you, I have nothing to lose. If I have a wife and kids, then I have something to lose. But right now I have nothing at all to lose. So if somebody toys with me too much, it might push me over the edge, and then anything can happen.

I'm pretty stealthy and get caught only once every three years. They had a sting for me last year at a yard in Minnesota. There were six officers, two dogs, but they didn't catch me. I beat them. They thought they were going to catch me, but they didn't realize somebody could get off a train at fifteen miles an hour without kicking dirt. Most guys wouldn't have done that. It's dangerous; you could break your leg or die. I can do it without kicking dirt. I was running alongside of the train, and I didn't hit the rocks. They didn't think I could do that.

They had a guy up on a hill staking the train out. He saw me and he gave me a dirty look. The train was two miles from the yard, and he radioed ahead to the bulls, who were sitting on both sides of the track waiting for the train to stop. I got off at fifteen, eighteen miles per hour. So I beat them.

I almost died several times. One time I was in a yard in New York. They knew I was waiting on the side of the bridge, and they kept speeding the trains up every time they saw me. But I got antsy. I was drinking coffee. Coffee is a bad thing for me. I've almost died twice drinking coffee. I grabbed on the train, between fifteen and eighteen miles an hour. I was running alongside of it just getting ready to pull myself up, going as fast as I could go. If he would have clicked it one more notch up, I would have kicked dirt.

As I was running along, there was a dip in the rocks, and I lost my footing. As soon as I lost my footing, I knew I was going to hit dirt. I hit the ground at about fifteen, eighteen miles an hour. I hit hard—rocks in my butt, rocks in my hands. But here's the thing—it never happened to me before. So it hurt my pride. I got up like a madman and I screamed. Aaaaaaaa! I was hurt. Blood was running down my leg, and my butt and hands were all torn up. It went right through my leather gloves.

I got up and I just went nuts. I grabbed ahold of one of those chemical cars, and I pulled myself up like a madman. I took my pack, which is a hundred pounds, and swung it on the grate and held on to the bar. I rode all the way from Albany to Pittsfield, Massachusetts. When we got to Pittsfield, I jumped off and got into a boxcar. I could barely walk to it. I always carry pain things with me just in case of an emergency. I popped one of those into my mouth, and I woke up the next morning in Boston. I ended up laying for three days, just healing. I hit hard, but at least I caught the train, so that was a good one.

The other time that was really, really bad was in North Dakota. This was probably one of my worst ones, probably one of the most stupidest ones I've ever done. I could very well have died, big-time. There was a train moving around probably fifteen to eighteen miles an hour again. I'm comfortable in grabbing those. It's dangerous, but I'm still comfortable in grabbing them.

There's a dead train right next to it. I caught the train before I got to the dead train. So while I'm grabbing ahold of it and running alongside of it, I went in between the dead train and the live train. But there's only a three-foot clearance in between them, and my pack is two-foot clearance.

Here again, I was just getting ready to grab the thing and pull myself up when here comes another dip in the rocks. I lost my footing. Ping-pong effect. Bing. Bing. Bing. The live train kept throwing me back into the dead train. It was moving fast, so I went boom, boom, I kept throwing back. Then I hit the ground and I rolled. I came this close to chopping my head off. I got up, and my heart's going ch-ch-ch-ch-ch. I stood there and let the train go by. I was scared to death.

The other time, I got stuck in a tunnel for forty-five minutes with no ventilation system. I have been riding a lot of years, and I have been through I can't even say how many tunnels. I've never been skittish about it, never had a problem with them. But now any time I go through a tunnel, I'm very "When's it over?" I actually went nuts that time. I panicked, and there was nothing I could do. I ended up taking my sleeping bag, wetting it down, putting it over my head, breathing through that.

That wasn't what got me. What got me was the darkness. Even with a flashlight, you know you're in the tunnel. You know it's dark. And I went nuts. I ended up passing out after ten minutes. I don't even remember it. All I remember is that when the knuckle clicked, when the train started moving, it jarred me, it woke me up, and I was praying that it wouldn't stop moving. When I finally got out of that tunnel, I haven't been the same since. I've been traumatized because of it.

I plan on being out here until I die. I hope I am, because it's helped me so much. Being on the trains has actually saved my life. I would have been dead years ago. I gave up on life. I gave up on life. I really wanted to die. That's what I mean when I said some things would send me over the edge. But I'm just going to go with it. I hope I get a wife and kids, too. God controls me, and he guides me where I'm supposed to be.

Hobo Advice

If you hang around hoboes long enough, you will discover that the advice they give is colored by their distinctive way of living. Here are a few hobo tips, gathered firsthand from those who learned them the hard way.

Never catch a train barefoot. —DANVILLE DAN

Be good to life or it will run off and leave you like a freight train leaves a tramp. —HOBO JOE

Don't get caught. —DANTE FUCWHA

Pray for what you want, but work for what you get. —ROAD HOG

Ride on till the wheels fall off. —FROG

Don't be in any hurry to get anywhere, take things one day at a time, look at every day as an adventure. Yesterday was an adventure, so tomorrow will be, too. —CAPTAIN CLOUD

When you hop on a train, you had better look up and down the track very carefully. Always hop the head of the car, and always ride three-quarters of the way to the rear of the train. The front of the train is going fairly fast when it enters a yard, and if you ride into the yard very far, you are more likely to get caught by the railroad bulls. —GREENIE

Never sleep with your back to the open. —WACKER

It's not good to be seen. —AN ANONYMOUS TRAMP

You gotta respect the train, because it's real easy to get hurt, and you'll never forget if you do, that's for sure.   —DIANA

Don't ride a train unless you know how to do it.   —OOPS

Always have plenty of water.   —CORRINA

Keep dry.   —TAZ

It's not a good idea to jump from a moving train with your backpack on, because you can tear up your face and get yourself killed.

—DRITS

There's a Little Bit of Tex in Me

HOOD RIVER BLACKIE

Some hobo poetry tells a story. The story in this poem reflects a theme in early hobo life—a younger boy connects with an older traveler, who protects him and shows him how to travel. Sometimes they stay together for many years; other times they part soon. Hood River Blackie crisscrossed America countless times with Tex Medders during the mid part of the twentieth century. After he stopped traveling, he still answered only to "Blackie" and not his given name. He died in 1984 at age fifty-seven.

Now I remember back during my hobo years
When I was footloose and fancy-free
I met old Tex down the railroad tracks
Camped underneath a tree

He was an old, old hobo
A legend from long ago
Who rode the freights in all the states
From Maine to Mexico

I knew old Tex always traveled alone
As he rode from state to state
But he broke his rule for a homeless kid
And we grabbed a northbound freight

Far across this mighty land
We rode where the wind blew wild and free
And I know as I look back through the years
There's a little bit of Tex in me

Skid row bars and railroad cars
And campfires down the track, oh man
Mulligan stewed and coffee brewed
Drunk from a blackened can

He showed me the Rocky Mountains
And we walked Death Valley's sands
He rolled his smokes from Bull Durham pokes
With his battered and time-worn hands

He told me tales of the hobo trails
And of adventures from long ago
About Chicken Red and Amboy Fats
And a tramp called One-Eyed Joe

And all about a ramblin' man
Who rambled from sea to sea
And you'd know at once if we ever met
There's a little bit of Tex in me

I guess I thought like Old Man River
We'd just keep rolling on
But twenty-five years went by so fast
I didn't know where they'd gone

So one fine day in the month of May
At the age of ninety-four
Old Tex went to live in a rest home
And could roam with me no more

Then the world seemed big and lonely
As I roamed the land alone
The grass wasn't green and the sun didn't shine
And the wind even seemed to moan

But I traveled on and my hair turned gray
As I lived the life that's free
And now more than ever you'd have to say
There's a little bit of Tex in me

But time goes by and all things change
And just the other day
I met a homeless, hungry boy
Down along the Santa Fe

He was dirty and tired and sick and sad
He came from the Lone Star State
And, you see, me and him kind of hit it off
So we grabbed a northbound freight

I'll show him the land and the jungle camps
And we'll go and camp by the sea
For I know it's true, and so do you,
There's a little bit of Tex in me

Iwegan

Iwegan is quiet, but full of conviction. He belongs to the "Boxcar Boys," a small group of long-time travelers who have a place in Minnesota they can go to when they are tired of traveling.

If someone tells you that the life of a fruit tramp, harvest tramp, hobo, is a life of ease with no responsibilities, they are out of their gourd. There is a certain sense of freedom, but it sort of goes like this: if the farmer don't pay you, there goes a part of your summer wages.

—Oklahoma Slim

I had a good mom and dad, but I was raised by my grandmother. My grandmother's husband, at that time they called him a rounder. He was a professional, but he rode trains. He wasn't so much a hobo, but they called him a rounder. I think he's the first one that I really realized that people didn't have permanent homes, but traveled around because that's what they loved to do. The old hoboes, they're gone now.

The old Rock Island used to come through my hometown, and the old hobo jungles I was taught not to be afraid of. I used to sit in the jungles when I was ten, eleven years old. I took my first ride at Freeport, Illinois, when I was sixteen, just for something to do. Then I hitchhiked across the United States shortly after that, and by the time I was nineteen years old, I had hitchhiked all the way to Eugene, Oregon. I caught a train from there, and I been pretty much riding trains since I was nineteen years old. I'm forty-four years old now.

I actually got off the rails at nineteen. I tried the citizen route and worked for a couple of years. I been out here steady since 1980, when I was twenty-four. About five years there, I went back home and did some things. Then I came back out here, and I been out here ever since.

I'm not limited in where I ride—I pretty much travel coast to coast. I consider myself a highline tramp. I'm physically unable to ride in the winters up north anymore, because I have bronchitis and I believe it's turning into emphysema now. So I stretched my itinerary. I go down to Gulfport, Mississippi, Brownsville, Texas, Pensacola, Florida, in the winters. There's nowhere in the United States I won't ride. I'm not a regional rider. No, I ride everywhere.

I think as you get older, instead of sitting still a day, you sit three days. I don't ride as hard as I used to. My last trip this year was, we were up in St. Paul, Minnesota, in May, and we came all the way down to Texas and then through Texas and over to New Mexico and into Utah, back over through Montana, then back to Iowa. I've been in sixteen states between May and August this year.

I usually try to keep a record of where I've been and how many miles and stuff in my journal. I try to do at least fifteen to twenty states a year. I think I've been a million miles, because seven or eight years ago, we used to run to Spookaloo a lot. Spooks—Spokane, Washington. That's fourteen hundred and fifty-five railroad miles out of the Minneapolis yard, so I say it's fifteen hundred miles. If you round-trip, that's three thousand miles. I used to run that eight times a year, ten times a year, just that, and then everything else, too. In a good year I think I'd ride fifty thousand miles. So I might have a million miles out here.

I had a lot of friends in Spook. A lot of it was riding back and forth. We'd go out to Wenatchee, pick apples. At that time I had a lot of work in Spook. That was just the neighborhood I was running. I had the same kind of network in Minneapolis. I used to winter in Minnie. I used to like to spend winters up north, but I can't do it anymore because it's just too darn cold for me.

I'm kind of limited in the work I do, because I was born with cerebral palsy. So I don't have the skills. I wish I could go to work for fifteen bucks an hour, framing or doing the kind of stuff my brothers do. I don't have the vocational skills; my motor skills are just not there. I will work day labor, I'll do whatever it takes. Sometimes I work for private individuals that I've known. I know people I can go back to in a couple of years. It's hit and miss.

What keeps me going is the freedom. The freedom is the utmost thing—the ability to be able to go where I want and to make my mind up about what I'm going to do, not have anyone over me. I've always been an individualist. My mom knew I was going to ride when I was a kid.

I call society snivilization, because everybody's running around sniveling. They got their wants and needs mixed up. All I need is a meal every day, some water on the train, a little bit of tobacco. Wants are nice, but as long as I get what I need, I'm going to make it. All these people in snivilization, as I call it, they're running around, and it seems like to me that they have all the material trappings and they're still miserable. I don't trust them. I don't think they have my best interest in hand.

I think that one of the biggest things that keeps me going out here is the brothers I run with. They have my best interest in hand. They're not going to lie and cheat. They're not going to tell me nothing that's not true. Society as a whole, I think, is phony, crooked, and something that I don't really want to partake of.

It's an ongoing thing sometimes keeping my spirit now. It's changed so much out here—most of my brothers are gone. Every time I turn around, it seems like I'm more of a lone soldier. But I'm going to stay out here till the roof falls off, if I can. I don't think I can ever get off. Sometimes that's a curse, but that's where it is. I'm a hobo till I die.

I don't travel alone so much anymore. I used to travel alone all the time. I'd stop and see my brothers a couple days and get back on almost always by myself. I could do exactly what I wanted to do then. Some of my interests are kind of different—I like to go to museums in cities, and I stay in libraries a lot. I'm about half afraid to ride alone anymore. It's foolhardy to think that you can, because it's not funny out there. There's too much crap happening. It's real good to have somebody watch your back.

I ride with people I've known ten or fifteen years. My brothers have kind of bonded together, the ones that are still out there, the ones that we know real well. We pretty much come together to watch each other. This last traveling we did all over the United States, I rode with my brother Patches. We've known each other nineteen years. As long as we're out there, we're going to pretty much stay together.

I think the violence out here reflects society as a whole. It seems like a lot more that they consider us throwaway people. There's been a lot of violence directed to hoboes in the last year or so. They had seven killings of hoboes in two nights in Denver last year. And they were nineteen-year-old kids, eighteen-to-nineteen-year-old kids, that were doing it. I don't actually know if these guys rode trains, but they were camping out by the yards. My brother, Dogman Tony, got shot in Iowa this year by a nineteen-year-old kid. He'd never spoke to him; there had been no altercation in camp or nothing. This kid had seen the hoboes in the camp and decided from a hundred yards away with a rifle that he needed to shoot a hobo. You can't make sense out of that stuff. That's scary, really scary.

At night I usually go down by the river. I'll go find the old hobo camps, where I think guys stayed years ago. Even if I'm in the city, I'll go way out, usually to something that looks like an old camp. I try to stay out of big cities. I don't like big cities. I think they're cesspools. The last few years, I've been running around in the Midwest. People seem to have a lot of good heart there. I've been staying in Kansas, in Missouri, and Iowa, just doing the little towns for safety reasons and for kindness. Big cities are like Sodom and Gomorrah. Human life ain't worth nothing anymore in the big city. I won't stay on the street. I refuse to. I'm a hobo. I stay in hobo camps. I stay down by the river. If I'm going to be somewhere for a little while, I might try to build me a little hooch.

Sure, I get tired of hoboing. I'm tired now. It's a cycle. I might be tired now, next week I won't be. Something'll happen that'll make me move again, something that I couldn't have unless I was out here. And that's what keeps me going, I think, is when I turn around, I see uniqueness. There's things that I take joy from that I couldn't get anywhere else.

I've had some real bad experiences, too. I got arrested, not this last January, but the January before. We'd all been celebrating New Year's Eve in Arizona, in the desert. I'd been drinking, and I probably had more than my share. I went ahead and laid in my bedroll, went to sleep. To this day I have no idea what really transpired. But there was a murder committed in the jungle. When the person got killed—this was told to me; I actually really don't know—he fell on me and landed on me fully. I'm sleeping.

The person that actually committed the murder took the knife and cut my hand wide open from my palm to my wrist. And they left the murder weapon in my pocket and stole my bedroll. So I woke up the next morning covered in blood from head to toe, with the knife in my pocket, which I didn't know about. I don't carry a knife, and I haven't carried a knife in fifteen years, because I drink and I won't carry weapons. If that gets me hurt down the road, so be it. I won't carry weapons. I don't want ever to have to say that I did something to hurt somebody, because I'm not like that.

They found the knife when I went to jail, because of course I didn't look for it, because there's no reason I would think that I would have a knife. So the murderer left the murder weapon in my pocket, stole my bedroll, left me covered in blood, and cut my hand wide open. I went to jail for first degree murder, for six months. They finally realized that I wasn't the person that did it. I never had to go to trial, because they exonerated me. They found the person that did it. It was a lady. They took her to trial, and she beat it. She beat a jury trial. She was found innocent. That was pretty frightening. I was realizing that I may go to jail for the rest of my life for something that not only did I not do, but that I didn't have no knowledge of. I don't have that ability to hurt somebody and do something like that to somebody.

My name's Iwegan. I've had that moniker probably almost twenty years. If you're from Minnesota, then you're a Minnesotan. If you're from Washington, you're a Washingtonian. So if you're from Iowa, if you're a citizen from Iowa, then you're an Iowan. And I ain't no citizen. I'm just a tramp from Iowa. I couldn't be Iowa Rick, because I'm not a citizen. I'm Iwegan.

They call me The Defective Detective also, because my father and my uncle and my grandfather, most everybody in my family that was males, were career law enforcement people. Everybody in my family were cops. About twenty years ago, I started telling my brothers that story that everybody in my family was police, and they says, well, then you got to be The Defective Detective.

I am a citizen. By being a citizen I mean that I'm not part of society, essentially. I don't like this government, I don't like what this country stands for. I love the United States. Only in America could I do what I'm doing. But as far as the government, I have nothing for them. I don't need them people. I had my social security for a few years because of my cerebral palsy, and they declared me to be physically unable and gave me my government social security. Then they turned around and took it away from me. I've been out here so long, and learned to be so self-sufficient, that I don't need their help.

When they took my social security away, they wanted me to have it, but they wanted a government agency to control it, like the Salvation Army or some kind of mental health program, and give me twenty dollars a week. I'm a grown man. I can control my own money, for one thing, and second of all, long before they gave it, I rode out here for fifteen years without food stamps, without checks. If they give me my social security check, it's something I can help my brothers out with. That's really what I'd used it for. It'd be gone in three or four days. Sure, sometimes drinking, but sometimes one of my brothers needed a bedroll. If my brothers needed something and I had that check, it was there for them. I don't need that.

I travel real light. I laugh at my brothers when they carry this hundred-and-fifty-pound high-tech stuff. I'm an old burrito tramp. I get me a big old plastic tarp, throw my bedroll and a blanket in there, get me a little kit bag. I don't carry more than maybe two days' food, two pair of jeans, a shirt, two T-shirts, and a long-sleeved shirt, maybe a bucket. That's all I carry. I got my water, I got my tobacco, I got my sleeping gear, I got a couple days food. It goes back to the wants and needs. I got my needs right there. That's all I'm ever gonna carry. Have burrito, will go.

The button on my hat says, "Foxes have holes, birds have nests, but the Son of Man has no place to lay down and rest." I have complete faith. No, that's not true. I don't have complete faith, but I'm working on having a complete faith all the time. Jesus Christ is my Lord and Savior. My brothers have helped me very much spiritually, just the way we live. I don't feel that I'm of this world. I feel like I'm just passing through this world. I'm a child of God, I hope.

I know I'm dirty. I'm a drunk sometimes. But I don't believe you can live out here on the railroad tracks and be an atheist. I ask God what I'm supposed to do. I'm not deeply religious. I don't go to church; religion is a manmade term to me. Spirituality is what I go for. If I'm in a position and I can help somebody and I don't, then I'm not doing right. I'm walking through and riding trains and going through this earth, hopefully being able to be in a position to help people. That's what I want to do. That brings me joy, to help other people. I'm not trying to say that I'm anything, because I'm not. I am a dirty, ragged railroad rider. That's all I am.

A typical day is getting up by seven in the morning and having a fire and some coffee and hopefully some breakfast if we have it. It's all about hustling. One place it might be going to the day labor at seven in the morning. Next place it might be going to the dumpster to get breakfast, or going to the food banks. It's not about staying in camp, unless you really got lucky. There's times we might stay in camp two days.

I don't always know what I'm going to do every day, but I get out and just start kind of looking. It's basically putting yourself in a position to have opportunities. It always consists of surviving and bringing the necessities to camp. I'm a firm believer if you got four guys in camp and you send one north, one south, one east, and one west, we're all gonna come back with something good. If you sit in camp and twiddle your thumbs, and talk about "I wish" and "I need to do," that ain't never gonna happen. A typical day for me is getting out and seeing what God put there and seeing what's there.

I do different things all over. It depends on where I'm at, because different places have different things. A lot of times when I get fortunate, I like to see what's native to that place. I like visiting. I was in Chicago not too long ago, at the Museum of Science and Industry. I like to find things to do, fun things that are educational. That goes right along with being a railroad tramp. My curiosity is usually abundant. There's always too much more to see. Maybe that's my number one thing about staying out here—there's always something around the corner. I still gotta see a whole bunch more stuff.

Before I came out here, I was in jail a lot when I was a kid. When I first come out of jail, I was real bitter. If I'm honest with myself, I think I had a victim's attitude—poor pitiful me, blame everything on everybody else. I realized when I got on the road the kindness and generosity of absolute strangers. The road's made me realize that people are really good. It's restored my faith. I try to surround myself with good people.

I think if anybody spent a few years out here and chose to go back into society, they could be a very successful businessman, because you learn how to think on your feet, and you learn how to improvise real hard. You learn how to use things that maybe you just discarded. We make things, we're very creative. It goes back to what I said about faith. I wake up sometimes with nothing, relying that the day's going to be good.

Roll Call of the Departed

Every year at the memorial service for deceased hoboes in Britt, Iowa, the names of those who have caught the westbound are read. The westbound is the train that carries hoboes to the "Great Hobo Jungle on the other side of all the stars." The Texas Madman compiled the list of names. Here are a few of them. The first fourteen are buried in the cemetery at Britt.

The Hardrock Kid
Mountain Dew
Slow Motion Shorty
Connecticut Slim
The Pennsylvania Kid
The Man Called John
Lord Open Road
Cinderbox Cindy
Fishbones
Hafey Zale
Cardboard
Hobo Herb
Slim Jim
Texas Bob
Admiral Dewey
Philippine Red
Hairbreadth Harry
Scoopshovel Scottie
King David I
Doc Bell
Iceman Jim
The Philly Kid
Onion Jack
Cannonball Eddie Baker
Arizona Bill

Bigtown Gorman
Hobo Bird
Nevada Kid
The Drifter
Sonny Slim Chance
Hippie Joe
Reno Jeno
Trouble
Step and a Half
Dee
Lawrence of Minnesota
Modock
Debra Lynn
Pinky
Florida Boy Blue
Sparkplug
Chico the Kid
Just Jim
Chief
Northwest Wandering Star
Violet Jordan
Michelle
Pilot
Little Stevie
Big Mike

Horizontal John
Red Dog
Lizard
Depot Debbie
East Coast Charlie
Mouse
Gold Bell
Papa Smurf
Oklahoma Slim

Pebbles
Speedy
Ding Dong
Thirty Weight Earl
North Coast Blackie
Caroline
Rainbow
Boxcar Myrtle

A Hobo's Remembrance

LUTHER THE JET

Luther the Jet has sung this song a number of times at the annual
memorial service for departed hoboes at the National Hobo Conven-
tion in Britt, Iowa. When someone else dies, he adds another verse
or two. The song is a fusion of hobo realities with the old gospel song
"The World Is Not My Home" and is sung to the tune of that song.
Luther has been a sometime railrider since 1976, when he earned
a Ph.D. in French literature from the University of Wisconsin at
Madison. The hobo preacher mentioned in the twelfth verse is
Steamtrain Maury Graham.

This world is not my home, I'm just a-passin' through,
My treasures are laid up somewhere beyond the blue.
The angels beckon me from heaven's open door,
And I can't feel at home in this world anymore.

Oh, Lord, you know, I have no friend like you,
If heaven's not my home, then Lord what can I do?
I'll catch the westbound to that far and distant shore
'Cause I can't feel at home in this world anymore.

An old hobo sittin' in a shanty by the track,
Dreamin' of the yesterdays that never can come back,
And all the friends he knew in the years beyond compare,
Struck a note on his guitar and with his music filled the air.

He said, "Oh, Lord, you know, there's many just like you
That done the best they could with what they had to do.
They wandered through the woodland, o'er the hills and
    by the shore
Till they just couldn't stay in this world anymore.

It don't seem all that long ago I saw the Hardrock Kid.
Nobody got around out on the prairies like he did,

'Cept maybe Bigtown Gorman or that good old Mountain
    Dew,
Him and Slow Motion Shorty was the best I ever knew.

And, Lord, please remember our brother Hobo Bill,
And old Lord Open Road, somehow I see him still,
He rode around the country with a bindle on his back,
And he never let you down when you met him by the track.

The Pennsylvania Kid, he was cantankerous, we know,
But since he's gone, the fires at Britt have lost some of their
    glow.
So, Lord, please think on him when to your kingdom you
    shall come,
And on Hafey Zale and Charlie Tuna, loved by all and one.

Connecticut Slim and Sparky Smith, they stayed here in
    the jail,
Then along with Tumbleweed they rode out on the rail.
In all the jungles of the land their name and place were
    known,
So today we commend them to the saints before your
    throne.

A Man Called John and Iowa Bob always had a tale to tell
    around,
And when they hit the punch line their laughter shook the
    ground.
Gone to their native country, but we hear them still today,
And at length we hope to join them in our homeland far
    away.

Fry Pan Jack—what camp would be the same without his
    fare?
Sometimes it seemed he could make a meal from nothing
    but thin air.
A crumb boss and provider, and a hobo without peer,
On that long westbound freight train he has not a thing to
    fear.

The Buckeye Driller knew where the purest water could be
    found,
From Pettisville to Wauseon and Sryker—all around.
Now in that foursquare city may he see you face to face,
And drink the living waters from the fountain of your
    grace.

Don't forget that hobo preacher, his name we all must know
His eyes are blue as skylight, his hair is white as snow.
The light that fills his life is a beacon to us all,
When he's gone to his rest, then his words we'll recall.

He said, 'I sometimes have met a man I didn't like,
But if he ain't too ornery, just take him out the pike,
Set him down by the campfire and give him of your fare,
He might turn into the Savior before you're aware.'

'Cause Jesus was a hobo, the greatest one of all,
He said the feast is ready for them that hear his call.
What mansions are prepared, in raptured courts above,
For a hobo and a dreamer who can see this world in love?

The freight trains up in heaven, they all run on time,
The bulls are out for coffee, the saints can spare a dime.
I bet you'll find a steam engine right inside the door
That'll take you to the jungle with a loud and thunderous
    roar.

And there by the river, a great and glorious crew,
The boys'll all be fixin' a big celestial stew,
And dishin' up this banquet, says the hoboes' Lord and
    King,
'Come, ye blessed of my Father, and whomever you may
    bring.'

So, Lord, you know, we have no friend like you.
If heaven's not our home, then Lord what can we do?
We'll catch the westbound to that far and distant shore,
And we'll feel right at home in this world evermore."

Road Hog

After traveling for many years, Road Hog settled in California for about a decade, then moved to Utah. Though he is in his mid-sixties, he takes to the train now and then. Of his life on the rails, he writes, "Five hundred jobs and five hundred jails, a drifter of heart, mind, and soul."

Riding trains has not taught me patience. I still don't have any. But it has taught me persistence.
—Billy Gott

It doesn't matter what you have or don't have; life is all about attitude.
—Road Hog

As a youngster, I was in an orphanage in Boston—it was called the New England Home. When I was eleven, on a December day, I had the urge to be free, and I wandered away. I roamed around the Boston Commons and through all the cobblestone streets. There was an old down-and-out fellow who offered to buy me a hot dog and hot chocolate. He had holes in his clothes and in his shoes and was on skid row. Later on that day—this was my first trip out into the world—later on that day it was getting cold. I had no jacket on, but I could feel the heat of the subway station, of Park Street subway station. I knew there were trains that ran under the streets of Boston. Wanting to get warm, I walked down there, and of course I didn't have the dime fare in my pocket.

I literally just jumped over the transoms of the subway. They had an old fellow in a cage, and the old fellow, he's yelling at me, "Hey, come back, you didn't pay." I got on the subway and rode all night long—the MTA it was called. I fell asleep and got into a dream world. Part of my dreaming was, "Gee whiz, I like this train." The thought ran through my mind, "Someday maybe I'll get to ride other trains and see the whole country." Little did I know that five years later I'd be taking my first ride, freight train ride, up in the Pacific Northwest, with four old-time Great Depression–era hoboes.

I had worked in New York City a little bit at the age of fourteen, and had had a couple of jobs there. I had made my way down to Maryland, Baltimore, and on down to Florida. And I hitchhiked out west, across Texas. My first arrival into the West Coast was Los Angeles about the age of fifteen. I remember having a transistor radio with me. I got some work peddling handbills in downtown LA. They called it a walking man. You walked daily passing handbills door to door.

Now, here's the other scoop. I was also a juvenile still. I had had trouble with juvenile authorities previously, because I was too young to be out. One day I was over in Burbank, California, and between jobs I'd get a little bit hungry. I decided to check the dumpster out behind an Italian restaurant. I'm raiding the dumpster, and here comes the squad car, Burbank police car. They say, "What're you doing?" I say, "I'm looking for some dinner." They want to know how old I am, and they find out I'm fifteen years old. They say, "Well, we gotta take you into custody."

The following day I met this juvenile officer for the Burbank Police Department whose name was Al S_____. He had just had a baby kid about a month old; his wife's name was Gladys. Instead of me going down to juvenile hall in Los Angeles, he decided to invite me into his home. I didn't know this when I was walking from the police station over to the juvenile division. I was thinking maybe I could split from him and take off running. But I'm glad I didn't.

When we got out to his house, he says, "Did you have anything in mind when you were crossing that police station with me?" I told him the truth. I says, "Yeah, I was kind of thinking about splitting and taking off." He says, "Would you like to have a little running race with me?" I says, "Sure." He outran me. He could really go.

I stayed with him and his wife Gladys and did some odd jobs around the house, like yard work. Him and his wife were very nice people. They were Christian people, by the way. I consider myself nondenominational, but they were true Christians from the word go. Very nice people. They got a used bicycle for me to ride around that area. I was supposed to be with them until the state of Massachusetts sent the money to have me sent back to Massachusetts, because I was still a ward of the state of Massachusetts. Deep in my mind, I really didn't want to go back to Massachusetts.

One day they wanted to visit part of their family north of Fresno, California. They would drive up there, two hundred miles, to the little town of Kerman. It's in a valley, not far from Fresno, a small place, out in the country. We got there, and it was nice. But after being there a couple days, I says, "Boy, I'm two hundred miles from Los Angeles. This might be an opportunity for me to hit the road," because I knew when I got to LA, in Burbank, it was about my time for Massachusetts to have me sent back. I decided then it was time for me to make a move. So I did. I hitchhiked from their place, started heading up into northern California.

I hitchhiked up to the San Joaquin, near Stockton, and I got to Sacramento. I walked about—I think I walked right around twelve to thirteen miles, way on the outskirts of Sacramento, along the old Roseville Road. The railroad tracks was right there. And I come to this little town of Roseville, California. Sitting along a tree there and the track was this old fellow with a beard. He had a big bindle, bedroll, big pack, and stuff like that. I had never met a hobo before.

I sat down. He says, "Where you heading, kid?" I say, "I'm going way up north. I been hitchhiking." And I say, "I'm going to Alaska." He says, "Well, I ain't going that far." I say, "Where're you going? Are you a hobo?" He says, "Yeah, I've got a couple friends, too." He says, "You ever ride a freight?" I says, "No." And I says, "But I sure would like to." He says, "Well, I'll introduce you to a couple of my friends."

I met his friends. They all had big giant packs, and they had skillets and banjos, and pots and pans. These were all seasoned riders; they were all in their fifties and sixties. They had all rode during the Great Depression years. Some of them had even been married at one time. They invited me to go along with 'em, which I was honored by that. I told them I'd do anything I could to help out in the camp, which I did later on, as far as getting wood and stuff like that.

We were over by the railroad yards, and the Roseville police drove up. It was around nine o'clock at night, right after sundown. Of course I stuck out like a sore thumb. I'm with all these old hoboes, and I was so very skinny and I had that baby-faced look. They rolled over, and I go "Uh-oh. Here I go." They say, "How old are you?" And

I says, "I'm eighteen." They both looked at each other. They didn't ask me for no ID or anything. Then they asked the old hoboes I was with. They say, "Is he with you?" They say, "Yah, we're going to go up to Oregon, Eugene area, working the vegetables and what have you. The kid's gonna ride with us." He says, "Okay. Go on, but you all better be out of here by midnight."

We left right around that time. I seen the train make up. The old 'boes, they knew what track it was gonna make up on. The yard goats—the switch engines—would make the train up those times. They'd put the crummy on—the caboose—and then the big locomotives. When you heard the air hissing, it was time to get on—it was all coupled up. They had to put the couplings on by hand in those days. So I got on. It was in a boxcar. They showed me how to spike the door, not to get locked in. They grabbed a spike and put it in that door. We rode up to Dunsmuir—that was the first place I rode into. It was great.

I was sixteen then—the summer of '57. I was born in 1940.

I come to the hobo jungle in Dunsmuir, and they shared, they were very generous, these old hoboes were. They tore apart their bedroll and showed me how to make a bedroll by rolling up the blankets in plastic and tying it at both ends, and slinging it over your back. That's known as a bindle, a West Coast bindle. So I became a young bindle stiff.

I went to the jungle, a hobo jungle—that's a camp along the tracks, jungling out. They knew how to get the stew prepared, and this and that, and they were very kind. I seen a kindness there that I never saw in my life. Boy, I sat down to a really good meal. They just knew how to cook that stew like perfect—they had all the makings. I helped; I was the gopher kid. I helped get the wood, the water, and all that to bring to the jungle, because I didn't want to be a jungle buzzard. I wanted to do something to show my appreciation.

Then I asked them later on—we went to Klamath Falls the next day—I told the old hoboes, I says, "I'd like to find out some way I can contribute to this camp. How do I get money to bring stuff?" One of the old hoboes was wise to it. He says, "You know what, kid? Never be afraid to knock on doors." He says, "Just hang your work lug on them. If they turn you away, just walk away with a smile on your face and say, 'Thank you kindly anyway.'" He says, "After all, "there's no shame in walking up to someone and telling them that you'll do something in return for what you get." And he says, "If one door closes, another door will open. And they won't always be boxcar doors." This old hobo, he had given me words of wisdom right there. He says, "If one door closes, another door will always open." That hung with me the rest of my life. That first ride, that first adventure.

I went into town, into Klamath Falls. I had never tried to promote before as a hobo, so this was a real challenge. I knocked on the door of the bakery and the meat market, and I stumbled with my words, because I didn't quite know what to say, but it worked. It worked. I got some baloney ends and some doughnuts and this and that at the bakery. By the time I had gotten through, I had promoted a whole shopping bag full of grub, and I even had a piece of change in my pocket. I walked on back to the jungle, I felt so good, and the old 'boes looked at me and said, "Hey, kid, you done well!" We got a good stew that night, even had a little wine with it.

The next day we rode another boxcar. We went up to Eugene, the most beautiful ride I've ever had in my life, over the Cascade Summit, eleven thousand feet. It was on the top of the world, going into Eugene. It was the most beautiful place to ride you could ever imagine, into the Willamette Valley and Eugene.

Those 'boes, they wanted to hang out there in Willamette Valley and do farm work. They were all migratory workers, which made them real authentic hoboes. They'd been that way for years. But I wanted to continue my journey to Portland and Seattle. So I said goodbye to them. I shook hands. But I remember one of the old 'boes said to me, he said, "You know what, kid?" He said, "You seem to be material for the road. It looks like you got it in your blood." He says, "I'll bet anything the rest of your life you're going to be just like us."

That thought didn't really enter my mind too much. But in a way I kind of knew what he was saying. As I walked away, they all had a big smile on their face. That's a memory that will never leave. He says, "You got it in your blood. You got it in your blood." From that moment on, I was hooked. That was well over forty years ago.

I made my own way up to Portland. All kinds of things happened in that yard. Then I made my way from Portland, I rode the Billy Goat railroad for the first time—the Great Northern—to Vancouver, Washington, on up to Seattle. It was raining like cats and dogs there in Seattle, and I encountered my first railroad bull. I'm in a boxcar sound asleep. I'm sawing logs, I'm just exhausted. The bull wakes me up, the railroad policeman. He wasn't in uniform; he was wearing western clothes. He had a western hat on, blue jeans, and a flannel shirt.

He says, "Good morning." I woke up. And he says, "I'm the rail-road policeman." He says, "Where're you coming from?" I told him I was originally from Boston. He says, "How'd you get up here?" I say, "I met some old hoboes down in California, and I come up on my own." He asked how old I was. I thought I was going to lie to him, but I told him how old I was. I told him I was sixteen. He says, "Well, it goes like this. Freight trains don't go from here to Alaska. I'll tell you what. Have you had breakfast yet?" I say, "No, I haven't had breakfast." "Well, come on with me," he says. "I'm going to the diner anyhow." Doggone it, the first railroad bull I met took me to breakfast there in Seattle. Bought me a full breakfast, too, every-thing—eggs, potatoes, toast, coffee, the whole nine yards. Then he gave me a ride to the highway on the outskirts of Seattle and wished me luck.

I actually made it to Alaska. Then I came back to the U.S. main-land, then I rode some more trains. I even went down to see that ju-venile officer and his wife in Burbank. Told him how I had hoboed. They were glad to see me again. 'Course they were a little mad at me for running off. First thing he told me—I'd come in all smoky from riding the trains—"Get in the bathtub. Get in the bathtub."

At the age of seventeen and eighteen, I was riding trains hot and heavy—all over Montana and into Minnesota. I had it in my blood. It was just constant, because I had the real wanderlust. The more I rode, the more I wanted to ride. I was what they call a heavy-duty.

I learned about working the migratory circuit. I learned from conversation in the hobo jungles with the old-time hoboes where the work was going on, such as the pears, the peaches, the lemons, the apples, picking peas in Walla Walla, digging spuds out of the ground, gandy dancing, anything. That's what the subject of con-versation was in the jungles. I learned about the slave markets, too, the daily labor, which I got to doing in Chicago.

Years later, I was in Klamath Falls again, and there were some old-time hoboes in the jungle there. They said, "Did you ever think about having a nickname?" I said, "No, I never thought about it."

People always called me Slim then. They said, "You ought to have a name besides Slim." I said, "I just can't think of anything." They said, "We notice you like to ride that unit all the time, especially going between Eugene and K Falls." I said, "That is my favorite ride." They said, "There used to be an old black fellow in New York that they called Road Hog because he rode those locomotives." Locomotives are called a hog. They said, "We notice you like the road a lot." I said, "You know, I like that name." So that's how I got to be called Road Hog—named after the locomotive of a train.

One has to be very, very careful about safety. Once I didn't have a solid wedge in my door, a boxcar door. I was in Stockton. I woke up in the morning, and that thing was slammed shut on me. I said, "Uh-oh. Am I in trouble." Sometimes we do some things that are stupid. We don't have all of our faculties together sometimes. Anyone can make mistakes out there. I said, "Uh-oh, I am in trouble," because the heat was out there, and in a couple of days I'd be ripe. They'll be ready to get me. I said, "I'll sit right here and make my peace." Fortunately, I had a jug of water.

So I told myself just to take it easy and kick back and relax. I did exactly that. I sat down on the floor and gathered my thoughts. Then all of a sudden I heard a switch engine come down the track, a yard goat. It picked up my car and assembled it on another track where a train was being made up. I was still locked in, but the train was beginning to move. I noticed in my boxcar there were a couple sticks of lumber, two-by-fours. As the train rolled down the tracks, it threw a switch to where it shook the boxcar, and the door opened. I ran and grabbed the two-by-four and shoved it in the crack. I kicked my foot and got the thing open again. Oh, man, was I happy. If I'd been there a couple days, I'd a been ripe. It's little things like that, incidents like that, that you have to watch out for. There's always a lot of dangers that exist riding the rails.

I rode a lot in the fifties, quite a bit in the sixties. In between, I had a lot of jobs. Sometimes I'd work three or four months some-where. I had a little brief stint in the military service, in the Navy, where I got an honorable discharge. Then I handled different jobs, I did a variety of jobs. I worked in factories, but always the train was in the back of my mind. As soon as I got a road stake, I wanted to bum my way out west again and jungle out. My hunger to get back on the rails was overwhelming. So it was pretty much a steady life.

I did the migratory circuit all through the sixties, riding the freights. Then I slowed down a little bit through the seventies. I still rode in those years, but it was always off and on. I worked in cities like San Francisco. I worked in Chicago, a lot of work in Chicago. I worked in the Twin Cities, I worked in Denver, I worked in Seattle, I worked in Portland, I worked in San Francisco, Los Angeles. I starting slowing down in the seventies, the eighties. Even those years, during the course of the year, I was still doing a bit of riding.

Oh, no, no, no, no, I never got tired of hoboing. That was the best thing that ever happened to me. It gave me a life. Meeting those old-time great professional hoboes, it gave me a life. If that hadn't happened, my life could have been a total disaster.

What kept me going was the adventure. I wanted experience. I liked people. I wanted to meet a lot of good people. I wanted to explore, to see the country, to see different regions of the country. As a youngster, that was my dream. That was the dream I was chasing—the hunger for adventure, meeting people, and doing different things.

It was the greatest gift I've ever had. I got what I wanted. If I had to do it all over again, I would. I wouldn't trade it for all the tea in China.

Hobo Songs

Whenever hoboes gather, there is likely to be someone who composes songs. I have transcribed these songs from tapes. For information about Guitar Whitey and Hobo Liberty Justice, see pages 1 and 16, where the poems on which these songs are based appear.

Catchin' Out for Freedom

Words and music by Guitar Whitey

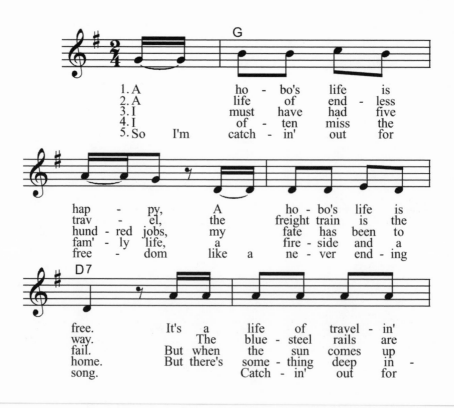

1. A ho - bo's life is hap - py, A ho - bo's life is free. It's a life of travel - in'
2. A life of end - less trav - el, the freight train is the blue - steel rails are
3. I must have had five hund - red jobs, my fate has been to fail. But when the sun comes up -
4. I of - ten miss the fam' - ly life, a fire - side and a home. But there's some - thing deep in -
5. So I'm catch - in' out for free - dom like a ne - ver end - ing song. Catch - in' out for

all   a - round,   and   that's   the   life   for
tell - in'   me: "Go   see   the   U.   S.
each   morn - ing,   I'm   head - ing   for   the
side   of   me   that   makes   me   want   to
free - dom,   I've   known   it   all   a -

me."   I'm   just   a   guy   who
A."   These   ci - ty   shack - les
rail.   Peo - ple   call   me
roam.   As   the   years   roll   by   I
long.   Ev - er   since   I   could   re -

won't fit   in,   I've   al - ways been that   way.   I'm
bind   me,   How I   long   to   get a - way.   The
"just a   tramp,"   a   "lo - ser,"   so they   say.   They
won - der   why   I   choose the   i - ron   rails.   The
mem - ber,   I've   al - ways been this   way.   I'm

catch - in'   out   for   free - dom,   I'm
high - line   is   call - in',   I'm
could   be   right,   I   put   up   no   fight,   I'm
ho - bo   life   keeps   call - ing   me   to
catch - in'   out   for   free - dom,

leav - in   to - day.   Catch-in' out for
catch - in'   out   to - day.
hap - pi - er   that   way.
fol - low   the   ho - bo   trail.
leav - ing   to - day.

free-dom,   I'll   soon   be   on   my   way.

One More Train to Ride

Words and music by Hobo Liberty Justice

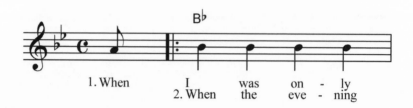

1. When   I   was   on - ly
2. When   the   eve - ning

twen - ty   one,   I   left   my   home   in
sun   goes   down,   I'll   find   a   place   to

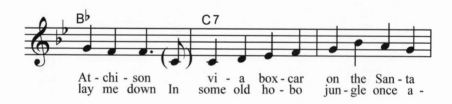

At - chi - son   vi - a   box - car   on the San - ta
lay me down   In   some old   ho - bo   jun - gle once a -

Fe.   Told   Mom   and   Dad - dy   not   to grieve, The
gain.   But   when   the train comes   by   at   dawn,   It's

time   had   come   for   me   to   leave,   The
"So   long,   pal,   I'm   mo - vin'   on."   I'm

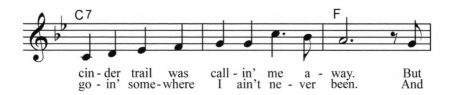

cin - der trail was call - in' me a - way. But
go - in' some - where I ain't ne - ver been. And

that was for - ty years a - go, I've
when I make my fi - nal run,

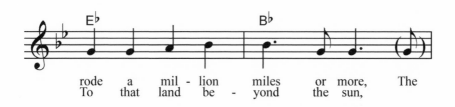

rode a mil - lion miles or more, The
To that land be - yond the sun,

ram - blin' fe - ver still burns deep in -
I will hold my head up high with

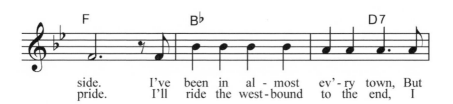

side. I've been in al - most ev' - ry town, But
pride. I'll ride the west - bound to the end, I

I could ne - ver set - tle down, I've still got that
hope St. Pe - ter lets me in,

one more train to ride. There's one more train to

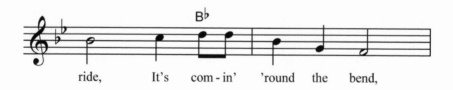

ride, It's com - in' 'round the bend,

Gon - na hop that old west - bound, Ride it

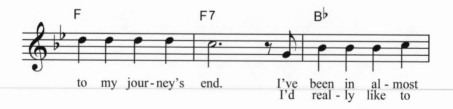

to my jour - ney's end. I've been in al - most
I'd real - ly like to

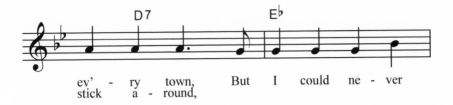

ev' - ry   town,   But   I   could   ne - ver
stick   a - round,

set-tle down,   I've still got that   one more train to   ride.

I've still got that   one more train to   ride.

Softly by Tracks

BUZZ POTTER

*Once the wail of the whistle gets into you, it won't come out. You will
stand by the tracks watching and waiting. You will reminisce about
your romance with the rails with a mixture of sadness and rapture.
Buzz Potter does this with much pathos in this poem. He was a
wandering worker as a teenager near the end of the steam era in the
mid-1950s. He died in 2003 at the age of sixty-five. This poem was
read by Garrison Keillor on* The Writer's Almanac, *a daily radio
program on National Public Radio.*

I stood by the main in the soft August rain
And watched as her headlight appeared
She crested the hill with a low moaning quill
Then proceeded through signals just cleared

She rolled down the main with a rumbling refrain
A song all the ramblers have known
The creaks and the groans and the low whistle moans
Remind us of yesterday's homes

Oh, how many times have I heard those old chimes
When my church was the high iron trail
When the vision of youth responded to truth
Expressed in a steam engine's wail

And the clunk of the gear brought a soft welling tear
As I stood there alone in the night
And I felt once again that deep yearning yen
That all us old ramblers must fight

Then she whistled a name that sounded the same
As a lover I knew long ago
I'd met her out there in the clean prairie air
In the rising sun's soft warming glow

I'd seen her at night in a campfire's light
I'd heard her soft call on the plains
I'd tasted her love in the rain from above
And slept with her often on trains

And the romance we knew I often review
And I savor the fond memory
Of the sweet cunning way that she led me astray
As soft as a south wind at sea

I remember her now but I can't recall how
I lost her and she slipped away
She sometimes comes back when I stand by the track
Then she sings and I must look away

And the rivers and streams still carry my dreams
Out where the long freighters roll
And the memories gleam as the lone whistle scream
Still calls to my wandering soul

As the years roll on by, I still wonder why
I miss her and long for her so
And her name in the end was freedom, my friend
A lover that most never know

The train passes by and there's mist in my eye
And it's not from the soft falling rain
And I know I'll be back to this place by the track
To watch freedom go by on the train

Raquel

Raquel is one of the newest members of the community of railriders and also one of the youngest. She has continued to travel off and on, both in the western and eastern United States.

So long. It is time to go, for I heard that lonesome whistle blow.

—Tumble Weed

I'm seventeen, and I started riding the rails about a month ago. I had been traveling before, hitchhiking, every break I'd get, in the summertime, whenever I could. I met these kids—"Oh, you should ride trains, it's safer." I was like, "All right." They took me on my first trip from a place in New York to somewhere in New Jersey, right by New York City, because I was trying to get down into the city.

I didn't have a sleeping bag, so I was cold. But I was really excited, because I had hopped it on the fly, and I had hopped off it while it was moving, too, which was not something people usually do on their first ride. It was a grainer—those are the easiest to catch on the fly. It was the coolest experience I've had in a long time. Now it's going to be more permanent. I'm going to be on the road for a good long time—years and years.

With hitchhiking, you're never too sure who's going to pick you up, especially when you're traveling by yourself. You can get arrested much more easily than if you're in a train yard. With trains, it's much more beautiful—you get to see backcountry, beautiful sights. It's way faster; you get to where you want to go like that [snaps fingers] if you get on the right train. I love the train, the way the train sounds.

I like it that you have to creep around. It's almost like a movie or something. You have to dodge the bulls, and once you get away with that, you got to find the right train. It's like problem solving. It's a little work and then it pays off. Gondolas are my favorite, because I'm kind of claustrophobic—it's open and you can stand up. You get really dirty in them, though, and you can get really wet if it starts to rain.

The scariest part about riding is that you don't know who'll be out there. Especially being a young female, you have no idea. There's people who'll take advantage of you if you let them know you're on that train. You got to stay out of sight, behind a big rock or behind a trailer or in some bushes or under a bridge. It depends on where the train stops. It's kind of hard, though, if someone else is catching it at the same spot.

Three days ago, with my friend, we're going to hop out of a yard in Wisconsin. We were walking toward the yard and we see this guy walking along, and she says, "Oh, look, it's a hobo." I say, "We gotta keep it careful." It was broad daylight. We walk up to him, and I got a creepy feeling. I know from hitchhiking, you look at someone's eyes and you can see they're a little bit crazy. He was very normal-looking, but he had a golf club that he kept pointing at us. He had just gotten out of jail, too.

The guy asked us, "Do you know where I can hitchhike out of here? I just got pulled off the train, and I can't go back there. I need to know how to get out of here." We told him. Then he asked us, "Where are you guys going?" I say, "Oh, we're just walking around." You don't tell people where you're hopping out from, because they'll be waiting there for you if they want to get you. I knew where to hop out from, but my friend said, "Where can we catch the train to Superior?" This was really stupid of her. This is the number one rule if you're a female traveler, not to do what she just did.

He gives directions. Now he knows where we are going to be. We go to the Subway, a food store, and get some food. Later on, I see him walking toward the yard, and I go, "Why is he going back to the yard if he's supposed to be hitchhiking?" We got all freaked out. But we had to get out of there.

Hours later, four hours, five hours later—it was late at night, pitch black in the middle of nowhere—we were going to the place we were supposed to hop out of. There's all these huge reeds and bushes and marsh at this one exact spot. We're setting our packs down, and he comes out of the bushes. He must have been waiting there for hours, uncomfortable in the marsh, to try to get us. We ran, ran, ran, ran.

I'm good at farming, I went to farming school for two years. I'm going to go to Colorado from here, work on a farm for about a week, get some funds, and keep moving, keep doing farming wherever I can. Sometimes I don't do that. I'm a cross between a hobo and a tramp. Sometimes I will fly a sign saying "Spare Some Change for the Sober," or something funny, and people give me money.

You can't take that much to get on a train. You have to let go of all your stuff. You learn how to live simple. It humbles you. Sometimes you have to stay in the yard for a week, and you don't know when you're going to get food, but everything works out if you believe it's going to work out and you have patience. It always works out.

We were in a yard in New Jersey, completely stopped there, and starved. One of those trucks that bring food to yard workers came. I went over to the truck and went, "Hey!" The guy was a Mexican, and I started speaking Spanish, "We're very hungry." He hooked us up with a tray of cheeseburgers and chicken. It was so much food; it was really good. You have some nice surprises. As long as you love what you're doing, it's all good.

I don't want to be inside regular society. It seems very boring to me to work nine to five to have money so you can get a big pile of stuff that you don't need. Some people are happy like that. I can't be happy unless I'm moving around. My father's a Dominican, and we'd go to the Dominican Republic, we'd go to Venezuela, and my parents would always send me away in the summertime. I went to different high schools, three different high schools. So I was used to not being settled. It's like I have a wander soul. I have to keep moving.

One of the biggest reasons I ride the rails is because I don't believe in working for the system. I don't believe in being in the rat race. I'm not into the politics of America, so that's why I believe in finding farms to work in and getting back to the land. The rails take me right where I need to go.

My mom finds it very weird that I travel by trains. She doesn't know why I am doing it. She's worried, just like every other mom, having an underage daughter riding trains and hitchhiking, but she feels safer me doing the trains than hitchhiking. My dad has no clue. We don't tell him anything, because he would go crazy.

When I'm sick, I go to a free clinic. I'm very good with herbs. I believe in natural healing. So I travel with an herb book that will tell you exactly what herb to use to cure. I bring things on the road like echinacea; it's always in my pack. I make everyone on the road with me take it. It boosts your immune system so you don't get sick. I travel with arnica for pain if anyone gets hurt. I carry homeopathic medicines for common things like a cold. If it's a cold or fever, I'll rest until it goes by, or I'll keep fighting it. I go and get an herb or food that will help me with it. I got stomach flu last summer from dumpster diving, and I got a bunch of ginger and ate it raw.

What keeps me going is needing to see things. The most fun I have is when I'm on the road getting to where I think the grass is greener. I always think the grass is greener on the other side. I get tired of being in one place for long.

I've learned that you can manifest anything you want. That's one of the biggest things. It's survival. You're out stuck somewhere, you say, "I'm going to get this." It's like a fight, a battle. I've learned to be like a warrior almost. You got to make sure you eat. I eat well, too, for being homeless on the road. And you can't lose hope, because if you lose hope for a second, you're gone.

You get back to your simple soul, your simple self, because basically you got to start over. Technology doesn't matter when you're out there. It's your survival instinct, your natural human instincts, that come out in every way—in dodging a psycho or manifesting some food when there is none or building a fire with very little things around. You learn to be resourceful, you learn to be alert. It's an art form, the art of freedom.

Death and Injury on the Rails

Death and injury on the rails almost always come unexpectedly, especially when they are the result of negligence. These accounts display both the danger of riding freight trains and the carelessness of some riders. Seasoned hoboes rarely commit such errors.

One of the first people I started riding with in the northwest on the highline was a man named BJ. We called him Step-and-a-Half. He only had half a foot, because he tried to catch a train drunk. He threw all of his gear up on the grainer and he went to step up, but he stepped on the track and the train jerked right over his foot. So when you follow his footprints, you have a whole footprint and a half footprint, a whole footprint and a half footprint.   —NOMAD

My friend Frohog got his arm caught in a knuckle—the coupler between the cars. He was crossing a train and it jerked. He sat in the yard for twelve to fourteen hours with his arm stuck in the knuckle, and a yard worker finally ran up on him. He didn't have his arm amputated, but it atrophied out and is completely useless.

—DIANA

One of my friends lost both his legs from the knees down. He was coming into Sacramento and the train rolls right through the town, but it's going about fifteen to twenty miles an hour. He got off there because he wanted to get off there, but he got off going too fast. I don't know if his ankles snapped or he lost his footing, but he got sucked under the train. It ran over his legs and cut them both off, one just above the knee and the other about three inches below the knee. He drug himself over the ballast and into the street, without his legs. Someone saw him and called the ambulance. He got taken to the hospital, and he was in ICU for two weeks. He's still alive, but he can't ride trains anymore.   —OOPS

I was sitting in the yard in Tracy, California, one time, and this old guy told me about a young guy just starting out. He told him about not running around and playing on the freight cars, they're pretty dangerous. The kid said, "Oh, I know what I'm doing." About five, ten minutes later, they heard a bloody scream, and they jumped up to see what the screaming was about. The kid had crawled down the ladder on the end of a car and had started to jump over to another car. He got his foot caught in the couplers and couldn't get it out. Took his foot right off.   —HOBO CHARLIE

I got hit in the face with a brick from a moving train. I was running alongside a boxcar, going to get in, and this guy in the boxcar stepped around out of the dark and hit me in the face with a brick. He could have just said, "I'm in here," and I would have got a different ride. That changed my mind about being a trainrider for awhile, but it passed, and I got my wanderlust back.   —NOMAD

The first time I ever rode a freight train was during a hot spell in July. I and my partner got off the train in a railroad yard about 2:30 in the morning. We picked up our gear and started walking along the train so that we could find another train that would take us to our next destination. Just as we started walking, someone got off the train about fifteen cars away and walked toward us. He was not carrying anything.

As he approached us, we could see that he was scruffy-looking. His clothes were dirty, he had a week-old beard, and his hair was unkempt. When he stood in front of us, we could smell the alcohol on his breath. He was also rather distraught.

His riding partner had fallen off the train before we had gotten on, and he wanted to know what he should do with his pack. I asked him how it had happened. They had been on top of the car, he replied, and his partner had fallen asleep. The motion of the car had gradually jiggled the sleeping rider toward the edge. Just as he was about to fall off, our informant had tried to restrain him, but had not succeeded. The sleeper fell to the rocks below as the train wound its way through a deserted section of a midwestern state. I had clocked the train at forty miles an hour.

I asked the person why they had gone up to the top. "It was hot," he replied. It was, indeed, hot—about ninety degrees and humid.

The car the two were on was a graincar. Graincars have ladders at both ends that can be climbed easily, and they also have two narrow catwalks on top. Each catwalk goes the length of the car beside the rounded hump in the middle of the car that also goes the length of the car. This hump contains the hatches into which grain is poured. Someone who is asleep on top of the car would most likely be partly on the hump and partly on the catwalk. They could easily be jerked off by the side-to-side swaying of the car. On normal track, railroad cars sway a little, and on rough track, they sway a lot, sometimes lurching.

We did not have any good advice for the distraught rider, other than to search the pack for an address and notify the people there. We left, wondering how long the rider would lie beside the tracks before he was discovered.   —TRACKS

The Road to Nowhere

DR. POET

Hoboes often have a destination in mind when they get on a train,
but sometimes they move just to be moving, going nowhere in
particular. Dr. Poet rode in the late 1980s and early 1990s. He has
sung at hobo gatherings and has produced albums of hobo songs.
This is one of his songs.

Heading down the road to nowhere
    Only wasting time
Heading down the road to nowhere
    On the South Pacific line

It's the last day of summer
    And I've got the urge to go
Heading west toward the setting sun
    Before the ice and snow

The lightning hits the iron road
    The wind is wild and free
The other side of the rainbow
    Is what I'm trying to see

Heading down the road to nowhere
    Trying to find my way
Heading down the road to nowhere
    No place I want to stay

I'm something like a winging bird
    Who never built a nest
Caught a mountain breeze one day
    And never stopped to rest

Adman

Adman traveled for a year and a half in his early twenties, partly by hitchhiking and partly by rail. His experience did not cause him to lament, but to find himself. He is now nearly fifty and the owner and chief executive of an advertising agency in Minneapolis. He still hits the rails for a week or so every year.

It doesn't matter how you get there if you don't know where you're going.

—Roadmaster

You can't be late to nowhere.

—Adman

I had some hard stuff happen to me in my early twenties, and I hit the road for one reason—to run away. It was to run away. That was more than two decades ago.

About halfway through that time, I was coming over from Portola, California, across the desert. My train had been delayed, and I ended up spending half a day in the desert. I got to Salt Lake really dehydrated and tired. So I spent the day making ends meet and getting some water and food and getting some stuff straightened out. I caught a piggyback late in the afternoon, and we shot up along the western Rockies, the western slope, making a cut up east into Wyoming, through Green River and then on up into the upper desert across Wyoming.

That night—going up that cut and going in through the mountains where you're following the canyons and the sun has set early because the canyon is only a small slit in the sky, and it's getting darker and you're hitting those curves and the curves are squealing through the flanges—that's happening, and you're moving pretty fast for going up through a mountain canyon piggyback. And you got the piggyback rollup handles slamming down and slamming and slamming and slamming. There's a mixture in the air of diesel fuel and high timber, wafts of each coming in, and it's getting darker and colder.

I'm laying there and I get down into my sleeping bag, and I make myself a broken cracker sandwich and I have a little bit of Mad Dog with me left, and I eat my sandwich and watch the world go by, and there are a billion stars in the sky, and I was thinking, I was thinking, "I can't think of anywhere I'd rather be than right here, right now. And I can't think of anyone I'd rather be with than me right now."

I've always believed if you're having a good time, don't rush off. You're hurtling up through the channels and wild rushing rivers, and the stars are there—if you stare at them it makes you feel like you're not moving, but if you see the poles whizzing past you realize you're on a hotshot to Green River. The air is rushing down over you, and you're all rolled out in your sleeping bag, and you're down underneath there and you close your eyes and say to yourself, "I feel cozy."

I realized then that home for me was between my ears wherever I was, and it wasn't in a place anymore, because up till then I had two homes. I had a home in Minneapolis and I had a home on the road. That had a profound effect on me, because I knew then I was really at home again, and from then on I started running toward rather than running away. I'm there on the train, and it occurred to me that what I was doing was moving forward now. I'm not running away. Here's some things I want to do, some semi-commitments, and then going and doing them.

The fastest train I ever rode caught out of a yard in Pittsburgh, a mail train that goes through Chicago. It was a piggyback, and it was an easy snatch. I rolled out under the wheels and watched the sun go down and went into the night. It was a really cold night in the summer. There was a chill in the air, and the cold steel flatcar sucked all the warmth out of me.

I slept for a while, and then the train slowed—it always wakes me up when it slows, because it means there's some danger maybe or something. We were coming to a cutoff by Pittsburgh and they were shining the train, which meant that the cops were on both sides with their headlights shining the train looking for interlopers. I'm pretty good at hiding, so I got up under the wheels and went through that. Later the train slowed for a crew change, and I ditched it and went over in the weeds and waited till it took off again, because I figured if they're gonna search it they wouldn't find me.

The train starts to take off again and I go and nail it, my same car, and start riding through the night. Fifteen to twenty minutes later I notice that my water bottle, which was in my pack, had gotten a leak in it when I had gotten off. My sleeping bag and my jacket, the two warmest things I had, were sopping wet. And it was cold. You're riding outdoors, the air channeling along the train underneath the wheels, absolutely cutting you like ice. And I've got the chills. I'm not sure if I'm shaking the train or the train's shaking me. It's one of those awful nights, and you count it minute by minute. You try to think of something else, but there's nothing else that you can think of than trying to hold yourself in a fetal position and hoping you don't die before you reach Chicago.

I must have slept a little bit because when I awakened, the train was slowing, coming into Hammond south of Chicago. I don't like to ride into Chicago because I've gotten ditched in South Chicago, and those neighborhoods are killers. It's pretty coming into Chicago, though, because as you're coming in, all the broken glass that's on the streets and in the neighborhoods and on the roofs sparkles. It's a sparkle that is a magical sparkle. If you look at it as sparkle as opposed to broken glass, you can see some of the beauty with the torture.

I got off at Hammond and let the train pass. I was stooping over as I was standing, still trying to ease out of the fetal position. When I walked across the tracks, it was like when you have leg irons on—you have to shuffle instead of walk. I was just so cold. I had my backpack over my shoulder, and I headed over to the other side. Up above me it was spaghetti junction, with cars going over for early morning traffic.

I saw a pile and I sat down in this pile, laid down my pack and sat down in this pile. The pile turned out to be wood chips. Now, wood chips, if they've been sitting someplace long enough, rot, and when they rot, what they do is create energy. A lot of times you'll notice, if you're gardening or something and you have your hand down in the mulch or you're putting your hands in wood chips, that it feels warm down there. And these had rotted quite well.

As I scooched myself back and forth to create a gigantic beanbag chair out of that pile of chips, it got warmer and warmer and warmer and warmer, and all of a sudden it took all the cold and sucked it right out of me. I could smell the fresh air of the morning on me, and I pulled out a cigar and I lit the cigar and sat silent for a moment. And then I said to myself, "Life is good."

Hobo's Lament

VIRGINIA SLIM

*A hobo can be so caught up in wandering that life's goodness passes
him by. At the end of the road, he may mourn dreams not found and
grieve for loves missed. Virginia Slim gives poignant expression to
this whole-life sorrow. When he traveled during his twenties, he was
known as "the spiritual wanderer."*

Oh, all the years that I have rambled
So many miles away from home
The dreams were vain, I never found them
I turn around and time is gone

I still can hear my parents' voices
Compelling me to stay at home
If I today once more could join them
I know I never more would roam.

Here in the darkness I can see her
It seems her voice is whispering low
A dark-haired maiden left behind
In the misty long ago

Gone down to rest beneath the grasses
And the chilly mountain dew
They rest in peace beyond the river
Those dearest hearts that I once knew

Across the tracks the moonbeams dancing
Oh, hear the somber whistle blow
The whippoorwill sounds so entrancing
As down the lonely road I go

Oh, all the highways I have traveled
Too many years from out my home
Life's pretty dreams, I never found them
I turn around and time is gone.

A Bindle Stiff's Last Ride

DRUMMOND MANSFIELD

*When the westbound is ready to go, you have to get on. It is a hobo's
last ride. Some have caught it young, and some have caught it old. If
you have time to reflect before you catch it, you will look back at your
life, as Drummond Mansfield does in this poem. He hoboed in the late
1930s, working the harvests up and down the West Coast, then later
became a railroad telegraph operator until the mid-1950s. He was a
professional artist until his retirement in 1980. The lines in his drawing come from "A Race of Men That Don't Fit In" by Robert Service.*

Huddled by a jungle fire
    This wet and gloomy night
Waiting for a rattler to depart
    Shiv'ring in my ragged coat
I am a sorry sight
    Enough to break my dear old mother's heart

But she has long been in her grave
    Thank God she'll never know
How I have fallen through the cracks
    And am an old hobo

I left my home in Arkansas
    So young and wild and free
I worked on every kind of job
    Wherever I happened to be

The call of a far-off place
    The desert, the mountains, the sea
The wind and rain in my face
    On a fast rollin' freight was for me

Romances came and went in my life
    Responsibility
Was something that I couldn't face
    I had to be totally free

The westbound now is blowing
    There's no place I can hide
Everything has a price tag
    And I'm takin' my last ride

Drawing by Drummond Mansfield

REFERENCES

There are numerous books and other resources for those who are interested in delving into hobo culture at more length. Here are a few.

Allsop, Kenneth. *Hard Travellin': The Hobo and His History.* New York: The New American Library, 1967. Contains a bibliography.

Graham, Steam Train Maury, and Robert J. Hemming. *Tales of the Iron Road: My Life as King of the Hobos.* New York: Paragon House, 1990. The life story of a million-miler.

Gypsy Moon. *Done and Been: Steel Rail Chronicles of American Hobos.* Bloomington: Indiana University Press, 1996. Contains life stories of twelve older hoboes.

Uys, Errol Lincoln. *Riding the Rails: Teenagers on the Move During the Great Depression.* New York: TV Books, 1999. A companion book to the documentary film *Riding the Rails.*

Iowa Blackie's book of collected poems can be obtained for $10 plus postage by writing to him at PO Box 487, New Hampton, IA 50659.

One More Train to Ride, the tape that contains Hobo Liberty Justice's "One More Train to Ride," can be obtained for $10 plus postage by writing to him at 8425 Sterling, Raytown, MO 64138.

Luther the Jet's song "A Hobo's Remembrance" is on his CD of train songs, which can be obtained for $15 plus postage from No Guff Records, PO Box 1235, Nevada City, CA 95959, or at www.utahphillips.org/tapecd.html.

Guitar Whitey's book *Ridin' Free: Short Stories of Steam and Diesel Hoboing* can be obtained for $12.95 plus $5.00 S&H from Zephyr Rhodes Press, PO Box 1999, Silver City, NM 88062, or at www.zrpress.com/ridinfree.html.

Websites

www.hobo.com   Contains information about current hobo life plus links to other hobo websites.

www.worldpath.net/~minstrel/Hobolink.htm   Contains numerous links to other hobo websites.

The Britt, Iowa, hobo convention is held the second weekend in August every year. The phone number of the hobo museum in Britt is 641-843-3867.

CLIFF WILLIAMS has taught philosophy for more than thirty years and is currently teaching at Trinity College in Deerfield, Illinois. He has published a number of articles and book reviews in professional journals. One of his books, *Free Will and Determinism: A Dialogue* (1980), entered its ninth printing in 1999.

Rye Cooder
    Texas Style

Tony Sandate:
    "Los Peregrinos"